SHORT CIRCUIT

ABOUT THE EDITOR

Vanessa Gebbie's short fiction has won over forty awards, including prizes at Bridport, Fish (twice), Per Contra (USA), the *Daily Telegraph* and the *Willesden Herald*, from final judges such as Zadie Smith, Tracy Chevalier, Michael Collins and Colum McCann.

She is a freelance writing teacher working with adult groups, at literary festivals and with school students. Her work with disadvantaged adults led to the publication of two anthologies of their writing: *Roofless* and *Refuge* (QueenSpark Publishing 2007). In 2009 she was invited to contribute to *A Field Guide to Writing Flash Fiction* (Rose Metal Press, USA), a creative writing textbook that received a coveted starred review from *Publisher's Weekly*.

Many of her prize-winning stories are brought together for the first time in her collection *Words from a Glass Bubble* (Salt, 2008). A second collection, *Ed's Wife and Other Creatures,* is forthcoming. She is Welsh and lives in East Sussex. For more information, see: www.vanessagebbie.com

Writing as Vanessa Gebbie

SHORT CIRCUIT

A GUIDE TO THE ART
OF THE SHORT STORY

EDITED BY
VANESSA GEBBIE

SALT

LONDON

PUBLISHED BY SALT PUBLISHING

Fourth Floor, 2 Tavistock Place, Bloomsbury, London WC1H 9RA United Kingdom

Salt Publishing 2009

Printed and bound in the United Kingdom by MPG Books Group

Typeset in Swift 9.5 / 13

ISBN 978 1 84471 724 8 paperback

1 3 5 7 9 8 6 4 2

CONTENTS

SHORT CIRCUIT

A GUIDE TO THE ART
OF THE SHORT STORY

VANESSA GEBBIE
INTRODUCTION

Welcome to *Short Circuit*, a collection of essays and interviews from winners of some of the most challenging competitions for short fiction — the UK's National Short Story Award, the Bridport Prize, the Fish Prize, the Fish Short Histories Prize, the Asham Award, the Commonwealth Prize and many more. Writers who also teach writing.

Short Circuit is either a very good title for this book or a very bad one. It depends how you look at it. I see surprising connections, sparks and flares — more than a modicum of the unexpected. However, those who know about electricity tell me it is a bad title. Because you only get short circuits if there has been a mistake in the wiring. Something unplanned.

I'll stick with it and hope they don't mind. And by the end of the book, I hope you'll see why it works well. So many of the writers here will tell you of the elusive and magical 'thing' that happens when story takes off and all your planning and plotting and learning of craft fades into the background. When your characters take over and use your fingers to tell their stories.

1

Here, you have craft issues discussed in context by twenty-four writers. If you are reading this book you are probably already writing short stories, and want to do it better. So do I. So do we all. We share with you our love of the short story form, and talk about what it is that we find challenging. Sure, we talk craft — about opening and ending a story. About characterisation, voice, dialogue, and shaping a story. About theme. Creating a world, settings. But we also share with you our creative processes, the strategies we employ to unlock those little bits of magic that are stories. We share ideas for further exploration of the processes described, and give you lists of inspirational stories.

I will leave you with two thoughts. Firstly, from the chief short-lister of the Bridport Prize, Jon Wyatt. When I asked him what he was looking for in stories that made the shortlist, he said he gave his team of readers a simple instruction. 'I want to see those stories that make you forget you are reading.'

And secondly, this, from an interview with William Faulkner in *The Paris Review*, Issue 12, 1952.

> Let the writer take up surgery or bricklaying if he is interested in technique. There is no mechanical way to get the writing done, no shortcut. The young writer would be a fool to follow a theory. Teach yourself by your own mistakes; people learn only by error. The good artist believes that nobody is good enough to give him advice. He has supreme vanity. No matter how much he admires the old writer, he wants to beat him.

With those wise words in mind, I hope you may find some inspiration in this collection of essays. I hope too that you may find the stuff of debate, enabling you to get a little closer to your own creativity—no-one else's. But more than that, I hope it liberates you and challenges you to join us in our love of writing one of the most difficult, annoying, powerful fiction forms in existence.

GRAHAM MORT

FINDING FORM IN SHORT FICTION

In whatever way, and under whatever circumstances, the reader may link the different phases of the text together, it will always be the process of anticipation and retrospection that leads to the formation of the virtual dimension, which in turn transforms the text into an experience for the reader. The way in which this experience comes about through a process of continual modification is closely akin to the way in which we gather experience in life. And thus the 'reality' of the reading experience can illuminate basic patterns of real experience.

WOLFGANG ISER (*Modern Criticism and Theory*)

Readers ought to be a little wary of authors' accounts of their writing practice. They are invariably fictions that tidy up and give logical form to what might otherwise be seen as an unsatisfactory and untidy process, where the subconscious eruptive impulse and the conscious organising principle are mingled. But the fact that those accounts may not strictly be 'true' does not necessarily devalue their content — in fact it gives them the power of fiction to persuade and stimulate through a partial view that is afforded a particular intensity. Here's my account, with that caveat, using examples from my own work — and some shameless personal detail aimed to make it less of an abstract account of how I think about writing.

The first short fiction I ever read (by which I mean the short story here rather than the novella) was in the comics and comic books I subscribed to as a child and borrowed from friends. One lad, in particular, had a constant supply of *Marvel* comics through an older brother. I'm sure that one of the enduring influences of those comics was the use of *frames* that captured a visual image and moved the action forward in a sequence that resembled a ciné film with intervening frames missing. I realise now that frames equate to paragraphs in a story or stanzas in a poem — to move between them is to move across the white space of the page, which is often a period of implied time. The articulation of those comic strips was something to do with the motion of time within narrative, and with the way in which readers imagine absences.

The comic that I subscribed to had both comic strips and more conventional stories written in continuous prose. I soon became most interested in the story without pictures — or, rather, the story that created visual effects through words.

The local library was about a mile and a half away and the walk took me along the local river as it threaded its way between dye mills and weaving sheds. Then a climb through the graveyard, past the smoke-blackened medieval church, to the mock-Tudor, 1930's library. Books — more specifically their contents — lifted me out of that decaying Lancashire mill town to new places, people and relationships. Then with a shock of recognition, like the shock of adolescence itself, I found the work of Arnold Bennett, DH Lawrence and Alan Sillitoe. Their stories were set in the very industrial / rural borderlands where I lived. Literature had become both an escape from and a return to reality. But that reality was changed now, somehow infused with fictional presence.

I'm still amazed by the potency of text—the way typography on a flat page (which means nothing to those not enrolled into that particular writing system)—can have such power to transform experience. When you multiply that power into a book, then into a library, with its thousands of books and millions of written characters, you begin to understand our uniqueness as a species. Our success has reached beyond mere biology and is something to do with language and the way that we pass on our knowledge, understanding—and stories—regardless of the restrictions of time, space and mortality.

My early revelation, as D.H. Lawrence said of SONS AND LOVERS, was that the work I was reading was 'the story of thousands of young men (sic) in England today'. Such stories broke through the solipsistic, comic-book world of childhood and early adolescence and made me feel a connection to others. About the same time, my older brother returned home from his first year at university with a box of books from his undergraduate English Literature course. I began to read novels, poetry and short fiction voraciously, not only work from the UK, but Europe, America, Russia and beyond. What had seemed an incoherent and unimaginable world was gradually joined up through literature—through what we would now describe as a form of 'virtuality'.

The short story retained a special place for me. Novels, after all, were often organised as sequential stories or episodes. But the short story could be read in one go as I lay in bed at night with my old valve radio playing, giving off music and the scent of hot dust. There was something satisfying and stimulating about the form and it's not surprising that, after poetry, the first things I tried to write were stories. Furthermore, since writing heroes had supplanted comic-book heroes, I was determined to use my own experience as a basis for my work.

Several years and many jobs in mills, factories, hospitals and graveyards later, I had my first short story published in the Saturday *Guardian*—a piece about working in an industrial dairy in the North Yorkshire market town. Others followed, somewhat sporadically, since poetry seemed my main vocation. Then a fallow period, when short story outlets became hard to find, then, a few years ago, a much more focused return to short fiction.

Much of this new fiction developed from my interest in the narrative poem—either long poems or sequences. Switching from the rhythms of poetry to prose is never easy, but I realised that there was considerable crossover in the forms. Not only could my poems have a strong narrative content, my stories could borrow the rhythms, compression, imagery, motifs, patterning and concision of poetry. They could leave a lot out—trusting the reader to fill in—and they could, theoretically, be word-perfect. Just as I'd laboured over individual words and punctuation in poems, so I applied the same micro-editing to stories. But re-drafting was never a chore to me—it was where I found out what I was trying to say, where the first spontaneous pages of a story became more closely organised and *layered* through the choice of key narrative moments and resonant language.

I was always less interested in the grand sweep of narrative or 'twists in the tale', than in the moment-by-moment progression of narrative seen through a character's experience. If, as Philip

Larkin said, 'nothing like something happens anywhere'*, then there was something truthful about stories that eschewed a grand excitement for a quiet epiphany. I had become fascinated by time, how we experience it and how writers deploy it, privileging the depiction of consciousness over the depiction of events. All literature explores what it is to be human and alive and this was my way. I realised that stories could not only have a conscious layer where we engage with events in time, but a *sub-conscious* layer where references and imagery triggered a deeper reaction. The use of powerful colours in a story is a simple example of this technique, triggering a subliminal, even visceral response, in the reader—a method also used in film and photography.

Other influences on my story writing were the biblical parables with their difficult moral codes, African stories and the oral tradition (when I began to visit Uganda for the British Council), and writing for radio, which emphasised and dramatised the human voice as an element in narration and first-person characterisation. Parables also related to some of the key building blocks of poetry—*metaphor* where one thing stands for another and *metonymy* where a significant part represents the whole. *Allegory*, too, is possible, where one story actually represents another sphere of action. So the shortness of the story, rather than seeming like a compromise, meant that it could powerfully suggest, if not actually achieve, the complexity of a novel.

The poet Paul Verlaine once said that a poem is 'never finished merely set aside'. Stories were not just short in duration, but often incomplete: and not just because the craft demands endless revision, but because a story, like a poem, is *necessarily* fragmentary. They speak to our wider human experience by focusing on a

---

* 'I Remember, I Remember' (*The Less Deceived*, Marvell Press, 1954)

tiny patch or patches of time. What prevents short stories from becoming merely fragmentary — nugatory lumps of prose — is their ability to *engage* the reader.

The reader, I would argue, both experiences the story as it unfolds and *completes* it. Not in a systematic way in which a novel is completed (though it never is, it's merely fragmentary on a bigger scale), but in a speculative way that fleshes out the bones of a narrative. I also realised that shortness was not merely expedient — in fact the stories were more powerful because their very brevity enrolled the imagination of the reader. Furthermore, I began to see creative writing as a form of 'shared consciousness' —the text is left latent on the page in typographical form, and 'activated' by the reader. The result is an imaginative 'experience'.

The primary way that a story engages a reader for me is its appeal to the physical senses when evoking place (a 'sense' of place is literally that) or human characters. The fundamental appeal — as in those early comics is *visual* — but the rest of the human senses, smell, hearing, touch and even taste, can be powerfully suggested through verbal language. In fact, literature is the only art form that can achieve this synthesis, though usually not all at the same time. Here's a short passage from my story 'Resistance' set in World War II France:

> Gustave broke off some stems of lavender from the rock-border and rubbed them between his stubby hands. His fingers were shiny with oil where he'd whetted the scythe. Lavender smelled good. It smelled of the earth, it smelled of sex, like the sheets of their bed at home.

The passage is rich in visual detail and switches from an implied external view of Gustave to an implied internal as the scene appears through his eyes. Because of the 'free indirect style'—the assumption of intimacy without actually writing in the first-person—we see his hands from above and share his thoughts, connecting the immediate smell of lavender with a deeper, more intimate memory.

The other primary engagement with the reader, of course, is through the story itself: the sequence of events, how we enter it and negotiate the changes in time as the story develops and modulates between 'time zones'. The opening lines of a story involve other tricky decisions for a writer: tense (past, present or future), point of view (authorial, characterised, neutral), the level of intimacy (first, second or third person), whether the point of view is especially privileged and whether it is exterior or interior (commenting on the action or participating in it). The opening sentences have to establish all this quickly and succinctly. Put like that it sounds complicated! Here's an example from my story, 'The Prince', that attempts this:

> All summer the boy from the big house next door was dying. We saw his bandaged head flitting through the raspberry canes, saw him drifting like a sleepwalker across lawns where his father and mother watched him. Something was growing inside him, shouldering aside his life. He played slowly, prematurely aged, as if learning to be a child when it was already too late. We didn't know that he was dying then, but we sensed that we were near a great event.

In that opening paragraph several key things are established. The story is set in the past, but a sense of an apparent or implied 'present moment' of narration is also established. The story is written in the first-person and establishes a setting that the voice describes in intimate detail and has participated in. The 'big house' suggests a difference in social status and, although the story is set in childhood, the voice also suggests the understanding and experience of an adult. That's the conscious layer of narrative; but the language itself carries more subliminal meaning. The reference to sleepwalking and the 'flitting' motion of the boy suggest a world of ghosts, a movement from life to death via sleep, prefiguring the larger theme of the story.

It's obvious from those two short examples that any story has to take liberties with time. If we were to describe an event in 'real' time, then the task of writing would be eternal as we continued to experience time. There is much evidence to show that we experience what we think of as 'reality' just as selectively —there is too much experience to register it all and our consciousness would simply be overloaded. Here, too, memory and the subconscious play their role, so that our experience of *similar* experiences allows us to take short cuts. Even more radically, some neuro-scientists have strongly suggested that what we think of as reality is partly imagined:

> Dreaming and being awake are the next of kin, if not exactly the same thing. Basically the brain is a dreaming machine, it is the brain that generates reality, it secretes reality, so to speak and that reality is modulated, is limited by the senses.*

Scientists who investigate dreams have also drawn strong parallels between dreaming and consciousness, suggesting that only

* Professor Rudolfo Llinas, *The Mind's Eye*, BBC2, 1 August 2000

the presence of reality in the form of exterior sensation inter-rupts our constant dream state.

Those writers who say they never think about the reader are trying to make a point about their independence of practice, as if their writing has a kind of purity. Mostly, they mean that they don't consciously aim their writing at a particular audience, thereby avoiding association with forms of populist genre or 'designer' fiction (interestingly, short fiction is particularly rich in genres). But the act of writing does not exist as a separate act from the act of reading. As Alberto Manguel points out in his book, *A History of Reading*, the moment that writing was invented so was reading. Not only the act of reading, but the presence of the reader in the writer's head. Elsewhere, Manguel speaks of the writing being 'rescued' by the reader. In this sense, the writing simply doesn't exist without a reader.

Of course, that's a simplification of what happens when we make marks on paper or tap out a message on our computer keyboards. Even as I write this, I'm conscious that the acts of writing and reading can never be separated. To write is to constantly anticipate the next word. The instant that it appears in typographical form, we read it for correctness, location, consis-tency, etc. So the writing of any story, poem, novel, or even sentence is a complex mental/verbal performance. The crucial issues about writing—the need for a common language and a shared writing system, for instance—only come about when the author's 'other' (the actual reader) picks up the text. The act of writing is also based on a much deeper assumption than the compatibilities of language and writing systems—it is based on a sense of shared humanity, that what we have written will 'speak to' the reader's own experience and excite their synapses in the same way. Such identification may be only partial due to different cultural or social structures or due to the passing of centuries, but a story written two thousand years ago and translated from Hebrew via Greek and Latin into the St. James' Bible still has the power and veracity to move me.

As a teacher of creative writing, I've always been wary of a sense of orthodoxy creeping into my workshops. Writing is about liberty and a list of prescriptions or proscriptions has always struck me as a singularly dismal approach. Every work of literature invents its own unique problems and they can only be solved through the trial and error of a heuristic writing *process*. Theories of creativity or imagination seem to desert us at the point of composition when we forge those crucial formative opening sentences, from which we can never completely escape. But it's also important to stand back from the writing process in a more analytical way to ask what writing *is* and what it *does*— how two-dimensional typography has the power to create a virtual imaginative experience that is powerful enough to supersede reality. We read a story on a train and remember nothing of the journey whilst retaining powerful memories of characters, places and events that have never really happened. Developing your own sense of this counter-intuitive process—your own sense of praxis or 'poetics'—can be immensely valuable when reading and, crucially, revising one's own work.

 IDEAS FOR FURTHER EXPLORATION

I've already described my own reticence about creating guidelines for other writers. Writing exercises, like accounts of writing practice, are distortions of what practicing writers really do. But maybe there are some useful things to say.

- Read widely and read analytically for technique, working out what the writer is trying to achieve and how.
- Read classic as well as contemporary work, foreign as well as UK authors.
- Focus on the first moments of a story and see how a writer sets up a story and how they carry forward the elements of the opening words and handle time until the end.
- Write 'spontaneously' (no such thing, of course) rather than waiting for inspiration—even scribbling down a few words will involve key narrative decisions that can be developed further.
- Write from the senses to create a detailed and vivid sense of characters and setting.
- Meanwhile, don't worry about where the story is going or it won't progress. It's essential to get a first draft in order to achieve form.
- Now edit your story to remove as much superfluous detail as possible—allow the reader some space in which to imagine your story for themselves.
- If your story doesn't work, take some coloured pens and map up all the shifts in time to reveal inconsistency, unnecessary complexity, or contradiction.
- Experiment with tense, voice and point of view, re-writing the opening paragraph of a story to find one that feels right. Finding form in this way can often liberate you to keep going.

- Don't be stubborn about criticism. It's good to have self-belief, but act upon the criticism you know, deep down, is true.
- Become a reader of your own work by arriving at a distance from it. Don't be terrified of reading literary theory — it can't hurt you, but it can stimulate you, especially the phenomenology of reading.
- Develop your own voice and style, but remember that a good writer is a ventriloquist, so don't get stuck with 'pretending to be yourself' as Philip Larkin once said.
- Don't write anything you don't really care about — life is simply too short.

 ## REFERENCE BOOKS

It's almost impossible to recommend relevant reading without feeling that nearly everything has been left out. The stories here are 'classic' pieces that have been very influential, but you should read widely in contemporary work and listen to short stories on the radio whenever possible. The reference books relate to themes in my essay.

Alberto Manguel, *A Short History of Reading* (Flamingo, 1996)
David Lodge with Nigel Wood (eds), *Modern Criticism and Theory* (Longman, 1999)
Susan Greenfield, *The Human Brain* (Phoenix, 2002)

FAVOURITE SHORT STORIES

'The Dead'—James Joyce, from *The Dubliners* (1st World Library, Literary Society, 2004)

'An Odour of Chrysanthemums'—D.H. Lawrence, from *The Prussian Officer and Other Stories* (Penguin Classics, 1995)

'The Loneliness of the Long Distance Runner'—Alan Sillitoe, from *The Loneliness of the Long Distance Runner* (Harper Perennial, 2007)

'The Love of a Good Woman'—Alice Munro, from *The Love of a Good Woman* (Vintage, 1999)

'The Metamorphosis'—Franz Kafka (Kessinger Publishing Co., 2004)

'The Daughter of the Late Colonel'—Katherine Mansfield (Kessinger Publishing Co., 2004)

'Cathedral'—Raymond Carver, from *Cathedral* (Vintage, 1989)

For some contemporary African stories in print as radio podcasts: http://www.crossingborders-africanwriting.org/

You can find out all about short story prizes and competitions here: http://www.theshortstory.org.uk/prizes/

CLARE WIGFALL

'I HEAR VOICES'—NARRATIVE VOICE, CREATING A FICTIVE WORLD, CHARACTERISATION, OPENINGS AND LEAVING ROOM FOR THE READER

AN INTERVIEW

VANESSA GEBBIE: A good voice is one of the best tools for creating a believable world with believable characters, isn't it? You often use dialect to draw readers into your fictive world. Can you talk about that?

CLARE WIGFALL: 'The Numbers' would be an interesting story to start with. The location of the story was inspired by the Outer Hebrides, and it is written in a very specific voice, but I'll happily admit I was never trying to evoke a Hebridean accent. I have never been to the Outer Hebrides, nor heard the people who live there speak, but I am quite certain that no one would speak like my character Peigi. What was instead important for me was that the way she spoke would immediately evoke a place that was strange and new to the reader.

Peigi's dialect is totally fabricated—I just made it up. I used a few words of Gaelic, found by research—a few words dropped in early on helped to give me a grounding in the fictional place as well as her character—and then just fashioned her speech in a way that sounded 'right' to me. I wanted the voice to be unfamiliar, but I was very aware that I must not overdo it.

GEBBIE: Interesting. I love the voice, but then I've never been to the Outer Hebrides. I just fell into the fictive world you created, and didn't question. I believed it totally.

WIGFALL: As do the vast majority of readers, thankfully! But I know that both geographically and in terms of voice, there are definitely things 'wrong' if you are a purist. I have since come across people from the Outer Hebrides who say, 'But we don't speak like that . . .' and while I can understand their complaint, my answer is always, 'I never aimed at correctness. I just wrote fiction.'

The Hebrideans in fact speak a very pure English, you see. If I'd mimicked that, the voice wouldn't have the same transporting effect on the reader. Besides, Peigi's not speaking English, she's narrating the story in Gaelic, so trying to create their spoken English wouldn't have made any sense.

The thing is, I wrote the piece for myself, a long time ago. Just me and the story, in my bedroom. I just enjoyed creating the world of the story—an imaginary island—and living with the characters for a while. As I say, even though it was definitely inspired by the Hebrides, and I did a fair bit of research into the area, I consciously subverted the facts to fit with my fictional purposes. For that reason, I purposefully never named the location because I was very conscious that my island was my own creation. If I was writing history, or non-fiction of another type, then I would have approached it differently and been aware of the necessity to reflect something real. Fiction is not so constraining. In fiction, the field is yours to do as you want. And I am delighted to find that the story, written for myself, has been successful for so many people. I have to take the line, if it is convincing for 99% of the readers, then that's fine. You will never please 100% of the potential readership, and if you set out to try you would never write a thing! Fiction does not have to be 'correct'. It must be preferable to alienate 1% rather than the rest.

GEBBIE: I love finding out where the inspiration for a story comes from. Can I ask what led you to set a story in the Outer Hebrides?

WIGFALL: I read about an American woman who moved there in the twenties when she was still a young woman, lived there all her life, and who spent her time documenting the way of life and folklore of the people, as well as building up an important archive of their folk music and songs. Her name was Margaret Fay Shaw. What she did fascinated me, and initially I wanted to write about her in some way, but I didn't think I could do this without first visiting the area and doing a lot more research into her life.

Instead, what appeared over time was 'The Numbers'. In it you will find many well known motifs from folk-tale traditions, but whereas tradition leaves the motifs unexplained, the story shows how today's interpretation explains much of the mystery.

GEBBIE: Is your character Peigi in 'The Numbers' based on Margaret Fay Shaw in any way?

WIGFALL: No, not at all. But certainly Fay Shaw's writings about the people she met helped to develop Peigi in my mind. I have a lot to thank her for.

GEBBIE: **You mentioned 'not overdoing it' earlier. I know that when I started writing, what I thought was a brilliant voice was received with giggles many times, because it sounded unintentionally comic in the readers' heads. How do you avoid that?**

WIGFALL: I listen to everything I write. I want to know how it sounds. I stop frequently, and read each sentence out loud. I am searching for the right sounds, rhythms, and echoes. I am a real perfectionist, and that is no doubt why I take such a long time to write a short story! I am constantly tweaking and changing—if something doesn't sound right to me then I change it. So often, all it needs is a word or two dropped in for the reader to fix the idea of a different voice in their heads, and then they 'hear' that voice from then on as they read. In the very first line of the story I use 'ken' for 'know', flagging that this is somewhere Scottish, I hope, for most readers. But I had to laugh when some friends told me their initial thought was that it was a typo! Luckily, it only took them a couple more sentences to realise what I was doing.

I think it's also worth saying that even when I know exactly how people speak, I've learnt that it rarely works to write dialect verbatim, as it were. It just looks very strange, and switches off the reader. I have an example—a story written phonetically 'in a Newcastle accent'. Perhaps a reader could decipher it, as they can the Edinburgh dialect Welsh uses so masterfully in *Trainspotting*, but I fear they might begrudge making the effort for a short story, and by the time they started 'getting' the voice, the story would almost be over. I'm thinking instead of perhaps turning that one into a screenplay sometime. Leave it to the actors to interpret the script.

With fiction, I think the key is restraint. Especially in the use of dialects. With my story 'Folks Like Us' I used a lot of unfinished words, endings are dropped, and its part of the voice. The 'literary' and 'correct' part of me added apostrophes to all those words. But when I went back to edit, I saw that those apostrophes only drew attention to the writing rather than the story, so I took them all out. I took the writer out of the equation, if you like.

GEBBIE: Can you tell us something more about how you work at writing a short story?

WIGFALL: I'm very undisciplined, so I wouldn't say there's any formula by which I develop my stories, but they usually just begin at first as vague cloud-like ideas. Over a matter of time, months or years sometimes, the ones that want to be written continue to develop and grow, like a photograph coming slowly more into focus. Then I usually start by writing notes, telling myself what I want the story to be about and how I want to write it and also beginning to sketch scenes and characters. I write these notes 'free form', and just see what comes out, I don't self-censor at all at this stage. I think on the page, if you like. This helps the story to become more clear in my head. I continue with further notes about the background of the story, events that are linked to the main events. I write a lot down about my characters, as I find this is a great way to get to know them. I then dissect, taking things apart, and may pick out pieces to use, maybe not. There will always be pages and pages more notes than the finished story!

GEBBIE: Can you tell us a bit about creating characters this way?

WIGFALL: Of course. There's one technique I find helpful and which I've often used with students when I'm teaching. I give them a character profile to fill in which asks all sorts of questions about their character. Not so much about appearance, necessarily, but about the character's relationships, their hopes and fears. It asks what their earliest memories are, for example. I find that as you ask yourself these questions about your character, you find that you gradually get to know them. Usually there will be a point when the character walks off the profile page into the story.

Prior to that point the character is in a kind of limbo — they only half-exist, and if I used them too soon, I know they would only be two-dimensional beings. I hate picking up a story and finding that the characters are two dimensional and thin. If the writer doesn't have a sense of their characters as wholly rounded people you can be certain that the reader won't either.

GEBBIE: Like an iceberg? The writer has to know the character in depth, but only a small amount is needed for a story?

WIGFALL: Exactly. You don't have to throw everything in, but you do have to know them very well. I sometimes find that my characters sit to one side, not letting me know them properly sometimes, until something small appears. For example, I struggled with the character Johannes in 'The Parrot Jungle'. He was a hard character to get right, as he is very reserved. It was tough not to have him fall flat, as he holds back so much and yet, as the author, you want to convey, without being explicit, that there is so much going on under the surface. I remember I found him very difficult to write until the day I learnt that his children had a hamster called Rolli . . . that made him come to life. Such a little thing. But he suddenly became real to me, and was far easier to write.

And in the same way that Johannes didn't 'live' until I gave him that hamster, other characters don't live until I find the correct name for them. They just don't feel right, and I try out many different names, until one fits. All of a sudden the right name hits me, and then the character comes together and makes more sense. 'Of course! This is who you are!' It is a real turning point.

GEBBIE: How much do you rely on trusted readers when you are trying out your stories?

WIGFALL: At first I hardly showed my work to anyone. Almost all of my friends and most of my family read my work for the first time only when the collection appeared, even though I'd been working on the book for almost nine years. I trusted one writer, a good friend, to give me straight feedback, and he was always my first reader. I then had a couple of other friends I would sometimes show stories to if I felt there were questions I wanted to ask a reader, and also relied upon my editor and my agent who were there from the start.

A trusted reader is worth their weight in gold. It has to be someone close who will give you a real unbiased opinion. Readers who just say, 'That story was really nice!' are simply no good to you. Your trusted reader is not someone who is there to make you feel good, but someone who is prepared to say 'Hey, this character doesn't convince me', or 'Why did you make this happen? That's crap!'

Your trusted reader has to be someone who gets what you are trying to say and do. They have to understand where you are going, and be confident enough to tell you when you're getting it wrong.

My Dad is an interesting reader, in this sense. He is an incredibly slow reader and doesn't normally read fiction, so when I give him a story he takes my work to pieces, line by line—(you can see where I get my speed from!)—I once gave him a story of just 100 words, and he came back after time with 26 written points that he wanted to discuss about it! At that point I stopped showing him anything for a long while, but I've come to value him now because even though he reads so slowly and painstakingly that he often misses the overall point of the story, he's a very good critic on a sentence-by-sentence level.

When I was first writing, I was much more private about my work as it was something very personal to me that I was doing for myself. I was never particularly concerned about publication or about people out in the world reading my work, and even though I already had a publishing contract for the book it was very difficult to imagine that it really was going to be published one day and people might actually read it. I just wrote because that was my way of making sense of the world. But now I am far more conscious that people are going to read my work and I think that makes me more aware of the need for objective comment. Perhaps you could say I'm not only writing for myself these days. I don't think that's a bad thing. It's just natural, it's something you have to accept if you want to make writing your career.

GEBBIE: Back to the voices you use. We were talking about how you don't have to be precise. Can you say something about how you create your choice of voice?

WIGFALL: As we said before, a writer of fiction doesn't have to be an expert in linguistics. You just have to convince. And to a certain extent it's up to the reader as well, to read closely, picking up all the nuances. So we are back to dropping in the odd word early on, the odd grammatical construct that differs from the usual. Some voices are familiar, and others are relatively alien. I've always been very interested in the way people speak and have a good ear for accents, so I think that's why I like writing with different voices. Often the choice hasn't been a deliberate one, it's more like I just start hearing the voice in my head. That makes me sound crazy, but it's how it works.

I can remember one particular instance very clearly. This was back when I was doing my Master's degree. I was lying on my bed and I had this voice going round and round in my mind. I went through to my friend's room and told him, 'Okay, this sounds really weird, but I've got this *voice* in my head.' He asked me whose voice it was and I said, 'I think it's Clyde Barrow.' So he urged me to go back into my room and start writing it down. What resulted was the story 'Folks Like Us'. Clyde's voice is a real drawl, drawn out sentences, slow. The sentences run into each other. Not much punctuation. I actually wrote it originally with no full stops, then went back some time afterwards and put some in.

It was strange though, because I'd never had any particular interest in Bonnie and Clyde before, so I don't know why his voice came into my head. Also, once I started doing more research, of course I realised that the voice I'd heard clearly wasn't some supernatural channelling of the dead Clyde Barrow because my facts were all wrong. As the story goes along, the facts align more closely with truth because I knew more by that point. I did wonder whether I should go back and change the beginning, but in the end I decided this was my story, and this was *my* Clyde so he could tell the story however I wanted. As I said before, I'm not aiming for correctness, I'm writing fiction.

Of course once the book was published and I started to have to give readings from it, I suddenly realised how much harder I'd made it for myself by writing in all these different voices. For readings it poses a real challenge, because I never know whether to try for the accent and risk sounding like an idiot. I've done it on occasions with some of the stories, and sometimes even if I read a story with my normal accent the voice comes across a little because of unusual words or grammatical constructions, but there are still voices I haven't dared try. Clyde being one example. I just don't think I'd convince if I tried to read as a Texan male!

GEBBIE: **You say to drop the odd word in early on. Can you talk for a moment about opening the short story? How do you approach yours?**

WIGFALL: I don't think there is a norm. Some of mine begin in the middle of the action—*in media res*—whereas others are recounted in a much more traditional way. I love to experiment, try everything out.

But openings are so very important. My editor has told me he can usually tell by the end of the first page whether something will be of interest to him, often from the very first sentence!

So I would advise anyone to really work on that first sentence. Make it really special. Pull your reader in straight away and give them something to care about as soon as you can. Your first sentence should raise a question. And lead you on to the next sentence, which either raises another question or deepens the first.

GEBBIE: Great advice. And is there anything else you'd like to say about writing the short story?

WIGFALL: I'd like to say a little about not trying too hard to tie up all the loose ends. About leaving room for individual readers to come to the story with their own take on things, giving them room to interpret your work as they will. In my work a lot is left out, deliberately. If things are not meant to be part of the story, I leave them out. So although I have everything in the story for a reason—I love leaving a trail of clues—I do not expect every reader to interpret my story in the same way.

For me, it's also very important to think about stories at the level of the word. When I write, there is not a single word I do not think about. As I said before, I read everything out loud, over and over again, tweaking phrases, sentences, vocabulary, and constantly paring down the story until I am entirely happy. I think always when you write, but especially when you are working on a short story, it's an exercise in saying what you want to say with absolutely no more words than is necessary. That challenge is something I love.

FAVOURITE SHORT STORIES

'A Perfect Day for Bananafish' — J.D. Salinger (in *Nine Stories*, also titled 'For Esmé — with Love and Squalor', Penguin, 1994)

'Hills Like White Elephants' — Ernest Hemingway (you'll find this in most collected editions of his stories)

'The Walls are Cold' — Truman Capote (in *The Complete Stories of Truman Capote*, Vintage, 2005)

'Tricks' — Alice Munro (in *Runaway*, Vintage, 2005)

'Nights at the Alexandria' — William Trevor (maybe this is a novella, not really a short story, but it's beautiful and you can read it in one sitting so I've decided to include it — I have an edition given to me by the author in which it is bound alone published by Modern Library, 2001)

'The Ant of the Self' — ZZ Packer (in *Drinking Coffee Elsewhere*, Canongate, 2005)

'Whoever Was Using This Bed' — Raymond Carver (in *Elephant & Other Stories*, Collins Harvill, 1988)

 IDEAS FOR FURTHER EXPLORATION

CLARE WIGFALL'S CHARACTER PROFILE EXERCISE
PREAMBLE: AN EXPLANATION

Here is a character profile that I've given to students when I was teaching. In those instances, they were given an original characteristic as a trigger, so you could work with a friend and make one up for each other, or you could just ignore this and fill it in for a character you have in mind.

There's absolutely no necessity to answer every question, or even to work through them in any particular order. Some will inspire you and be more appropriate to your character than others. Sometimes you just might not know the answers yet. And you might be surprised that it's while you're answering one random question that a story is inspired.

Another fun thing you can do if you're working with someone else is to actually swap character profiles at the end and write up each other's character, although you might feel too protective of your creation to be willing to do this!

CHARACTER PROfiLE

Your name:

Original characteristic:

- What is your character's name?
- Age?
- A brief physical description (e.g. height, facial shape, hair colour, spectacles/contact lenses, distinguishing features)
- Typical outfit to wear?
- What city/country/location do they live in?
- What is their home like?
- Method of transportation?
- Kind of education?
- Do they have a profession?
- Who is the love of their life?
- Are they in love with anyone now?

- Do they feel content with life?
- Do they have a best friend or someone they confide in?
- Did they have a happy childhood and what were they like as a child?
- How is their relationship with their parents?
- Do they have siblings? If yes, are they close?
- Do they have children? If yes, what are their ages and names?
- Have they ever lost anyone important to them?
- What is their speech like? Any distinguishing characteristics?
- What is the thing that most worries them?
- What thing is most important to them?
- Is there anything that they are frightened of?
- Has their heart ever been broken and how?
- If yes to the last question, are they over it now?
- When were they happiest?
- Where would they most like to visit?
- Favourite food?
- Hobbies?
- Does he/she have a pet? What kind?
- What does your character most hate?
- What are their obsessions?
- What is their long-term goal in life?
- What do they dream about?
- Do they have any secrets?
- Do they believe in a religion?
- Do they believe in life after death?
- Was there any significant event that changed the course of their life?
- What is their favourite colour?

- What kind of music do they like to listen to?
- What would they order at a bar?
- Do they like to dance?
- How well does your character get on with other people?
- What five characteristics would somebody who knew them well use to describe them?
- In what ways are they like you?

Additional notes:

_____

_____

_____

_____

_____

_____

_____

ALISON MACLEOD

WRITING AND RISK-TAKING

'd be lying if I said any different: the short story is big. It matters. It matters too much for me not to be honest—which is why I've been sitting here, hunched over my keyboard, hesitating. How can I give you something that does justice to the big-ness of the short story? How can I talk to you about the writing of short stories without talking away the mystery of the form?

I'd like to offer you practical, deep-running advice about short story-writing; we all need that if we're to midwife our stories into life. We all have to learn our craft and apprentice under writers who are either living or dead. But more than that, I want to say that every story that matters to a reader—every story that hums with a meaning greater than the sum of its words—was once little more than a risky act of faith for the writer. If there was just one thing I could say to you, it would be this: you don't get anywhere without the risks.

The legendary story writer Flannery O'Connor wrote many a radiantly insightful thing about the form but one remark, in particular, stays with me: 'a story is good when you continue to see more and more in it, and when it escapes you.' I like her emphasis on the escape, on the get-away, break-out, on-the-run, Bonnie-and-Clyde quality of a great story. I like the idea because something can only 'escape you' if it has a life-force of its own, and great stories do. Uncannily, exhilaratingly, they *live*. And that's what I want for you: a story that takes life beyond you, perhaps once you've sent it out into the world, or, even more thrillingly, as you write it. It's for that feeling above all—for the connection to that sense of mystery—that I write. It's a chemical rush to the brain. Some adrenalised truth is mainlined to the heart. When you read the last line of a great story, you realise you need to remember to breathe.

I started this essay trying to be honest with you. So I won't stop now. It has taken me a whole evening of being stuck, of not knowing where to begin—because, as I say, the short story, though obviously short, is big. I moved from boredom (drinking too much late-night black decaf and idling on the internet) to frustration (the pulling of hangnails) to small-scale despair (why did I accept this commission?). Initially, I thought I'd write you something elegant, something accessible yet authoritative. Then I decided I'd opt for wit and trenchant insight. Wit is tricky but, on a good day, it's not beyond me.

But *style* wasn't going to be enough. *Style* wasn't honest enough.

So I did what I always do when I give up on a piece of writing. I shut down my computer, turned off the desk-lamp for the night and ran my bath.

My bathtub is nothing special. Let me rephrase that. My bathtub is far from special. My weekly laundry dries above it on a 1930s rack that depends on a haphazard system of pulleys. An old transistor radio sits on the edge of the tub. Last night, I tuned into *Late Night Love*, courtesy of the local commercial station. I needed a loving dose of Brian Adams, Lionel Ritchie and Celine Dion. I'm not proud.

I scrutinised the adjacent wall for mildew, to which it is worryingly prone. I wondered, briefly, if mildew is in fact mould. Will my bathroom ever give me lung cancer? In the bath, I studied my stomach, trying to decide if it was fatter or flatter these days. I considered my nipples. Was it true what my sister had said: do nipples pale with age?

These are things I shouldn't be telling you. We're strangers. If ever we meet, I'd rather the image of me in the bath didn't flash up before your eyes—and I'm sure you feel the same. But I'll risk it because that's what writers need to do. They need to not be afraid. They need not to worry what people will think. They need to move beyond polite conversation. On paper, they have to be real. They need, at times, to explore what is supposed to remain covered; they need to say what might be unsayable or even unspeakable. Not in order to shock or to parade a gimmick. (Those stories won't last.) But because it's often the only honest way of telling a story—of getting to the elusive truth of things. I'm not the first to recall the words of Ezra Pound: 'Fundamental accuracy of statement is the *one* sole morality of writing.'

I am telling you about my bath because, unpromising as it is, uninspiring though the views are from my tub, it is the place where I am most often reminded of just how mysterious the act of writing is. It's there, once I've sunk deep, once I've stared at the walls and the peeling paint, once I've given up *all* hope of finding the right idea, line or image, that the right idea, line or image arrives, unbidden. It feels like a brush with something bigger than me, and it's something for which I'm always profoundly grateful. Of course there are other explanations—more rational explanations about the way the brain and the creative mind works—but stories have their own truths, truths that often exceed the known facts. As I stepped out of the bath, the first lines of this essay arrived: 'I'd be lying if I said any different. The short story is big.'

It is now almost two in the morning. I am clad once more. The pen is moving in my hand, almost by itself. Stories—even this one—get hold of the writer. They make their own demands. It's a strange thing to say, but again, I don't care about sounding strange. Or I do. I suppose I do. Everything would be too easy if I didn't care. But I care far more about saying something real about the writing of stories.

My hands hover above the keyboard. Am I sounding over-earnest? Over-zealous? Do I sound like a TV evangelist?

Don't think, Alison. Just write.

Imagine this. Inside the get-away car of your story, a comfortable silence settles between Bonnie and Clyde. He steers briefly with his knees as he opens a bottle of beer. She stretches her legs high, one at a time, and pulls off her dusty boots. She rests her feet on the dash and frowns at the hole in the toe of her worsted stockings. But outside the window, the world is budding green. Trees flicker past at forty miles an hour. Sunlight bounces off the hood of the car. 'Where's this story goin'?' she says, but she just says it for something to say. The truth is, she doesn't much care. She only cares about the prettiness of her legs and the way Clyde hauled her onto his chest that morning and the trees speeding by and the day that could go on forever. He flashes her a dangerous grin. 'Hell if I know.'

Because that's the first risk you need to take for your story. You need to be willing not to know. You need to be willing to let one sentence create or suggest the next. If you know everything you want to say as you start writing, the story won't be a story; it will be a message. It might be accomplished in many respects — fluent, well made, stylish even — but it won't have the energy it needs to survive. It won't have the sense of urgency, of intentness, that will make a reader care; that will make your story resonate with new life after the final line. Part of the gamble, the riskiness and the uncertainty you feel as you write is catalysed into the tension, the focus and the unfolding, live quality a good story offers its readers — whether that story is told in the past or present tense; whether it is subtle and restrained in style, or edgy and dark.

We should never feel sure that we can pull a story off. We should always be taking on a little more than we think we can manage artistically — driving off-road at times and without a map. The worry, the panic, the need to think on our feet, to develop our skill line by line, to live alongside the characters, discovering as they discover, groping as they grope — sometimes knowing more than they do about what's up ahead, sometimes less — all of this is the fuel that makes the story *go*.

Don't get me wrong. We absolutely need to study the craft, to pay our literary dues, to learn (and learn a lot) from the work of other writers, and to do all the above with humility. Every good story takes shape against all odds. There was nothing before, but now, behold, there's a whole world that can travel from mind to mind, from imagination to imagination, and say something about what it is to be alive and to be human. Who can understand the scale of that literary feat — and the craftsmanship it takes — better than another story writer? But at the same time, we should never try to educate ourselves beyond the sense that short-story writing is, at its best, an act of *not knowing*. Arguably, the story itself knows more than we do, and we need to train our imaginations to be receptive to its cues; to pay attention to the prompts that come only as feelings across the back of the neck, as single images we wake buzzing with, as lines we step with from the bath.

So the willingness *not* to know is the first risk we take as story-writers. There are others.

If I write a story about a woman who falls in love with her anaesthetist during a session of ECT, will my students/my neighbours/my employer wonder if I have mental health issues? If I write about a confused 19-year-old girl who finds herself erotically drawn to a dying (and subsequently dead) man, will my readers wonder if I was once similarly troubled? If I write about a fictional young couple who are affected by the London bombings in July 2005, will critics ask what gives me the right to create a story about a real-life tragedy I didn't directly experience? If I write about ball lightning that comes from between a woman's legs when she's aroused, will friends, privately, think I'm weird? If I write an experimental story that uses the structure of the outlandish questions that appear (in reality) on the American visa-waiver form, will I seem immature when I send the story to respected literary editors?

There will be good reasons not to write almost every story you care about writing. But it is a greater gamble if you don't write the story; if you pass it by for another story that risks nothing.

Which isn't to say that my students/neighbours/employer/readers/critics/editors won't think some or all of the above. Nor do I want to suggest that everyone — or indeed anyone — will applaud your risk-taking. Other writers might, but beyond a few kindred sorts, it's impossible to predict. Risks are risky for a reason. It's easy to look back after all has gone well and to think, wasn't I bold and ground-breaking? But there is a fine line that separates bold from just plain embarrassing, and it's hard to be sure of the distinction as you write, no matter how experienced you are. You can only take the risk and know two things: 1) that you are doing it for the right reasons (not for the sensation, the gimmicks, or the chance to preach or show off) and 2) that you have brought every bit of your talent, literary skill and energy to bear upon the task.

The task?

We're back to Ezra's 'fundamental accuracy of statement'. Accuracy of thought. Accuracy of emotion. Or, more simply put: honesty. Whether we're writing dirty realism or Dali-esque surrealism, we need to be true to life. That's the job.

But let's take the element of risk-taking beyond the author's imperative to write honestly. Let's also take it beyond the experience of story-writing by the seat of your pants. The risks, the gambles, the dares we take in life — or don't take — reveal who we are because they reveal what it is we truly want or need. They reveal the core of who we are. The same is true of the characters we create. A character *is* his desire, said Aristotle. But in fiction, as in life, that which we desire often comes at a cost.

A poem is many things, but it is fundamentally about language and image. A novel is many thing, but it is, above all, an architecture of events. A short story is language, image and event, but it is fundamentally about *character*. The *plot* of a short story is nothing more than an *unfolding* of a character, or perhaps the unfolding of a couple of characters. That's the beauty of the form, the terrific sense of intimacy it can offer us.

Somebody wants something. But something is clearly at stake for that character. His or her ability to attain the desired thing or person or outcome is blocked. Complications have arisen, both expectedly and unexpectedly, both in the world and, particularly, in the character him- or herself, as the story unfolds. But all of these complications (the plot, if you like) are really only there to show us, with greater and greater focus, the *desire* of that character and with that desire, the character him- or herself. A short story, said V.S. Pritchett, should capture a character 'at bursting point'. In a great story, the nature of a life is laid open — tragically, comically or absurdly — perhaps for the character him-or herself to see, but certainly, subtly, for the reader. In a moment of luminous insight that James Joyce of course called the 'epiphany' of a story and Joseph O'Connor has more recently dubbed the 'quiet bomb', we witness the truth of another life, and we understand.

Sure. It's easy for me to describe the 'zing' of a good story in a paragraph. It's harder to *do it* on paper in a story. I know.

I often find myself drawn to writing about characters who are attracted to something that is taboo. The taboo desire involves risk for the character, and quite often, risk for me as the writer. But I am grateful for the way the taboo thing, person or situation immediately creates a complex emotional world: one that holds the power of both fascination and shame, longing and guilt, or even fear. Contradictory feelings are jet-fuel for stories; they immediately give a story the tension of opposing emotions and they are also, in all their messiness, particularly true to life. Flipping through my notebook, I see I've jotted down the following ideas/images:

- A self-professed art lover stood trial accused of kissing a $2-million painting while wearing red lipstick and damaging the canvas.

- A surge in nude sleep-walkers among guests has led one of the country's largest budget hotel groups to re-train staff to handle late-night nudity.
- A Brighton taxi driver tells H. that his biggest fear is that a woman will take off all her clothes in the back of his cab.
- Ellen has no choice but to breastfeed Evie on a bench in the mall. A group of teenage boys stare, covertly, from a distance.
- At Christmas, Jack (5) takes the large cardboard wrapping paper tube, now bare of paper, clasps it between his legs and says, 'Aunt Jean, look how big my privates are.' Aunt Jean is 82.

Criminal actions are of course taboo, but most taboo actions are by no means criminal: swearing, top-shelf magazines, breast-feeding in public, laughter at a funeral, staring at someone on the Tube, talking too honestly at a dinner party, masturbation, the thought of one's parents having sex, kissing/smoking behind the bike sheds, etc. The kiss to the canvas, though illegal, was in many ways, so simple—an ordinary, if slightly mad, extension of the desire many of us feel at times to touch a work of art. The desire to break a taboo or the fear of a taboo being broken (as in the taxi cab driver's case) is most affecting in fiction when it is most familiar to us and most specific. The big criminal no-no's— bestiality, cannibalism, necrophilia—are all certainly taboo but, in all but the most experienced authorial hands, they're likely to swamp a story.

If, as writers, we can see, hear and touch the taboo thing/feeling/action/place/person to which our character is attracted, we can also begin to understand who our character is and where his/her story might begin. Why are they attracted? To what exactly?

What do they stand to lose? What do they feel guilt about or fear? Ask yourself each of these questions. I'll get bossier. Write a paragraph on each before beginning to write your story. Also, try to recreate on paper the allure of the taboo thing to which your character is attracted. A copy of *Playboy*? Someone's locked diary? The holy wine behind the church altar? Someone's mother's clothing?

Or was a certain place taboo, perhaps in your own childhood? The town dump where children were forbidden from playing? The staff room at school? The public loo of the opposite sex? Your parents' bedroom?

Was a certain person taboo, off-limits, or forbidden? A powerful person? A teacher? A priest? A woman after childbirth (in some cultures)? A lover? Why?

In a story that which is taboo immediately creates, firstly, desire and secondly, complications—the two essentials you need to make a story *move*. Whether the story is comic or serious, taboos suggest 'other sides' to our characters; they can reveal depth, complexity, double-ness, demons and secrets. In terms of plot, taboos create pressure, dilemmas—and a need to act, to decide. Our characters are tested by such complications, and as they are tested, they are more and more fully revealed to us, their creators, and, in time, to the reader. A need to act means a choice is made. A choice brings consequences and, in a great story, consequences often lead to a sense of revelation—that quiet bomb again. For along with the possibilities of shame, fascination, desire and fear that we are offered as writers when we risk a taboo subject, we can also, paradoxically, touch upon a sense of the sacred, which the word 'taboo' *also* suggests in all its etymological impurity.

The greatest story writers understand this. In Chekhov's 'Lady with Lapdog', the lives of Dmitry Dmitrich Gurov and Anna Sergeyevna are transformed by what was thought to be nothing more than an illicit holiday fling. Against all expectation, against the norm, the experience has been life-changing.

> And by a kind of strange concatenation of circumstances, possibly quite by accident, everything that was important, interesting, essential, everything about which he was sincere and did not deceive himself, everything that made up the quintessence of his life, went on in secret . . . He and Anna Sergeyevna loved each other as people do who are very dear and near, as man and wife or close friends love each other; they could not help feeling that fate itself had intended them for one another, and they were unable to understand why he should have a wife and she a husband . . . They had forgiven each other what they had been ashamed of in the past, and forgave each other everything in their present . . .

Chekhov is not recommending holiday flings. Nor is he suggesting that our real lives should be lived in secret. But he knows that story writers in particular need to look at the 'undersides' of their characters' lives; that stories are not sermons; that they can, if we risk it, open up to a brief view of life as it is truly lived; that, in the small miracle of the hard-won epiphany, a story becomes big and resonant; that, in stories, the taboo thing is often, finally, about life-force itself.

FAVOURITE SHORT STORIES

Each of these stories relates, in some way, to the idea of 'taboo':

'Lady with Lapdog', Anton Chekhov from *Lady with Lapdog
and Other Stories* (Penguin, 1969)
'Brokeback Mountain', Annie Proulx from *Close Range, Brokeback
        Mountain and Other Stories* (Harper Perennial, 2005)
'Lilac', Helen Dunmore from *Ice Cream*, (Penguin, 2001)
'Night Vision', Amy Bloom *A Blind Man Can See How Much I Love You*
        (Picador, 2000)
'Losing Track', Tobias Hill from *Skin* (Faber and Faber, 1998)
'After A Life', Yiyun Li from *A Thousand Years of Good Prayers* (Harper
        Perennial, 2006)
'Blood', Janice Galloway from *Blood* (Vintage, 1992)
'Meaty's Boys', Adam Marek from *Instruction Manual for Swallowing*
        (Comma Press, 2007)
'The Bloody Chamber', Angela Carter from *The Bloody Chamber*
        (Vintage, 1998)
'What We Talk About When We Talk About Love', Raymond
        Carver from *Where I'm Calling From* (Harvill, 1993)
'Johnny Panic and the Bible of Dreams', Sylvia Plath from *Johnny
        Panic and the Bible of Dreams* (Faber and Faber, 1979)
'Silver Water', Amy Bloom from *Come to Me* (Harper Perennial,
        1994)
'The Last Days of Johnny North', David Swann from *The Last Days of
        Johnny North* (Elastic Press, 2006)
'Weddings and Beheadings', Hanif Kureishi from *2007 National
        Short Story Prize Collection* (Atlantic, 2007)

'The Penis', Hanif Kureishi from *Midnight All Day* (Faber and Faber, 2000)

 IDEAS FOR FURTHER EXPLORATION

From Alison MacLeod's essay:

If, as writers, we can see, hear and touch the taboo thing/feeling /action/place/person to which our character is attracted, we can also begin to understand who our character is and where his/her story might begin. Why are they attracted? To what exactly? What do they stand to lose? What do they feel guilt about or fear? Ask yourself each of these questions. I'll get bossier. Write a paragraph on each before beginning to write your story. Also, try to recreate on paper the allure of the taboo thing to which your character is attracted. A copy of *Playboy*? Someone's locked diary? The holy wine behind the church altar? Someone's mother's clothing?

Or was a certain place taboo, perhaps in your own childhood? The town dump where children were forbidden from playing? The staff room at school? The public loo of the opposite sex? Your parents' bedroom?

Was a certain person taboo, off-limits, or forbidden? A powerful person? A teacher? A priest? A woman after childbirth (in some cultures)? A lover? Why?

NUALA NÍ CHONCHÚIR

LANGUAGE AND STYLE: A GUIDE FROM A SHORT STORY WRITER/POET

Writing short fiction and writing poetry are two different things; but as a writer of both I find that certain aspects of the writing of each can complement the other. Poetry requires brevity and concision of thought and language; so does short fiction writing. Short stories have a narrative arc, as do some poems. A good poem often contains an element of surprise, and a good story can too. In painting, Lucian Freud referred to this as 'a little piece of poison'. I love to see a little something poisonous, mischievous or odd in both poems and stories — it's what causes that shift of the heart that, as a reader, I hope to find in literary work. Another uniting factor in both these forms is the writer's dedication to language: both poets and short fiction writers are passionate about words and they want to put them together in beautiful and original ways.

All of the writers I know love language, word-play and articulacy. Their biggest kick in life is getting words to fall from their pen in beautiful, apt sentences; sentences that are well-crafted and that carry their story forward. Their aim, always, is to say things in fresh, exciting ways; to hone their writing style. They want to thrill readers with the spark and beauty of their prose. This is not to say that writers overload their work with flashiness for the sake of it: simple, clear, concise prose is as carefully crafted as ornate, poetical prose. Only you know what kind of prose you want to produce, and that may differ from story to story. What you want is the right words, to add colour and texture, to the right story.

If you want to write short fiction and write it well, see if you recognise yourself in the list below; if you do, you have the necessaries to write good short stories:

- You value brevity and concision in writing.
- You are convinced you have a talent for words.
- You read a lot, especially short stories.
- You are a good listener.
- You are nosy, an eavesdropper.
- You are sensitive and observant.
- You have been jotting names you like/snippets of conversations/observations about other people into a notebook, or onto beer-mats, for years.
- You have a good memory.
- You are a vivid dreamer, awake or asleep.
- You enjoy your own company.
- You can make the time to write, even if it means one less hour of TV per night.
- You are determined—a stick-with-it kind of person.
- If you don't already have a thick skin, you are willing to grow one.

- You are patient, or can learn to be.

There is no big secret to being a writer of short fiction or anything else, you simply must write. If you learn the sea by sailing it, then you learn to write by getting words down on paper. Every short story, poem and novel is written one little word at a time; one word after another. As Jack Heffron said, 'If you want to write, you must begin by beginning, continue by continuing, finish by finishing. This is the great secret of it all.'

The short story writer, like the poet, values and celebrates brevity: she is able and willing to get her story down using the fewest possible words. She is a happy editor: if something doesn't fit in her story, she is not afraid to get rid of it.

In order to be a writer of short fiction, you must also be a committed reader within that genre. Just because you are literate does not mean you can write a story. Words arranged on a page do not a story make. You must love the act of reading, particularly short stories. Your reading of accomplished work has already taught you writing skills, whether you know it or not. So, if you are not reading the classics, your contemporaries, or literary magazines, get going. Read everything you can—poetry, stories, articles, novels, non-fiction—you never know what tiny snatch of information will inspire a good story.

You must be observant: writers try to record with honesty their observations about humanity, the world and other people. It helps if you are a curious soul with a good memory. If your memory is not great—and even if it is—you must always carry a notebook and pen. Buy the tiniest notebook you can find—shirt pocket-sized, micro handbag-sized—and carry it with you always. When you are out and about, living your life, you will see and hear amazing things. Amazing things are great story fodder and writing them down for later use will be a major help to getting started, when you are faced with the dreaded blank page.

Writing is, by its nature, a solitary act. Whether you write full- or part-time, you will do it on your own. You can join a writers' group for feedback on your work, but the actual writing will take place with only you and your pen, or computer. So, it helps if you like to be on your own. I am a hermit. I like nothing better than being alone to write and dream and read. Conversely, I love company, but I save my socialising for the times when I am not working. Time alone is a privilege when you are a parent and partner and employee, and all those other things that we all are. But if you are determined to write, you must find that alone time in your day. That may mean getting up at 6am, or forgoing one of your favourite soap operas, in order to get words on paper. This is not a sacrifice; it's a gift to yourself. Tenacious writers often succeed in being published; stick with it and it will turn out right for you.

You must also learn patience, something I personally find hard. The publishing industry moves at a glacial pace. Stories and books are rarely accepted for publication overnight. It happens but it is rare; we tend only to hear about the rarities. For every success-story writer who receives a six-figure advance, there are thousands of writers still waiting one, two, twenty-five rejections later, to get published. Be patient.

WHAT IS STYLE?

The most durable thing in writing is style, and style is the most valuable investment a writer can make with his time.

It pays off slowly, your agent will sneer at it, your publisher will misunderstand it, and it will take people you have never heard of to convince them by slow degrees that the writer who puts his individual mark on the way he writes will always pay off.

RAYMOND CHANDLER

We all know what style is when it comes to how a person looks. It is easy to see who is stylish and who is frumpy, by their clothes or hair or jewellery. But what is style when it comes to writing? Well, it is the language used; choices with grammar and syntax; the pace of the prose, and the author's stance within the piece. If that all sounds like a school lesson, here's a comforting thought: you already have style. *Great*, you're thinking, *I don't have to work too hard at this, I've already nailed it*. Wrong! Yes, you have style but that is because, as John McGahern once said, 'In writing, style is personality'. Your personality oozes into your work without you knowing or being able to stop it. Everything you write is stamped with your innate style.

Think about Picasso for a moment; like many artists, he painted portraits. But it was *how* Picasso painted people — his *style* of painting — that makes his work Picasso-esque. Similarly, how you paint pictures with words is what makes your writing style unique to you.

You need not stay awake at night wondering about your style, whether it's good or bad. At its simplest, style is the way you use language and how you tell your story. Style is not added to the writing, like salt to soup — it *is* the writing. So style can't be taught as such (nobody can teach you to be yourself), but there are plenty of things you can do to make yourself a better stylist and, therefore, to improve your writing.

Style is the way a writer expresses herself; it's personal and unique because it is bound up in all that she says, is and does. Be true to yourself. Don't fear colloquial language, embrace it. Use the language of your childhood and home-place — use all those words and phrases that are part of your exclusive personal store and, therefore, your style.

Words are important. As a writer you are most likely in love with words and language and their possibilities. Story and character are obviously crucial in fiction too; the language is only the means to tell the story. But when words are used in surprising ways to tell a surprising story, there is nothing more beautiful for a reader. So adore words, bask in them, learn new ones all the time, and use them to tell your story in the best possible way.

You can write about anything you want, about places you have never been to and, by delivering it with style, you will convince your reader. Don't censor yourself when you write, let it all tumble out. Editing comes later.

As avid writer-readers we seek out certain writers because we like their style of writing. We then might sit down and try to write like, say, Annie Proulx but it won't work. There's only one Annie. So you have to be true to your own life, obsessions and vocabulary, and concentrate on talking about them to your readers.

I am so enthralled with visual art that for a while I feared I would become a one trick pony: a lot of what I wrote for the last three years involved paintings in one form or other. But I'm writing myself out of this at the moment; new and old obsessions have come to the fore again. The author Mike McCormack told me he nearly drowned reading my first collection of stories *The Wind Across the Grass* because it was awash with water. I don't write so much about water these days but it still appears from time to time. We like what we like.

Don't be afraid of the language that comes most naturally to you. Where possible, try to use language that's true to you and that flows from you. Don't rewrite every sentence ten times, always scrabbling for the perfect word or phrase; that's struggling. Give yourself the freedom to free-write and you'll see that sometimes the first thing that pops out will be the truest to your own voice and style. What appears from your pen may surprise, upset or disgust you; sometimes it might even make you happy, but whatever it is, it's uniquely yours and that is something to cherish.

Read your work aloud to check for fluency. I do this all the time; my kids think I'm mad. Try reading the sentences slowly, or staccato, so that you don't miss any words. If it sounds bumpy to you, it may to a reader. Tone up the lumps and bumps by shortening sentences, or changing the word order. Get rid of anything that is not a fit.

You may have heard the phrase, attributed to Mark Twain or, sometimes, William Faulkner, 'Kill your darlings'. I'm uncomfortable with that: if your 'darlings' are the best bits, why on earth would you kill them! You will learn to recognise the difference between when you are writing well and when you are showing off or adding in things that are not relevant. The show-offy writing will make you feel a tad mortified when re-read; the good bits will give you a soft, inner glow. Pick your darlings carefully. Kill only the show offs.

HOW TO TIGHTEN YOUR PROSE AND IMPROVE YOUR STYLE

- Use normal rather than obscure words. e.g. 'chew' not 'masticate', 'building' not 'edifice'.
- Practice brevity and edit well; say it succinctly. e.g. 'I quickly ran, as fast as I could, to where she sat.' Instead: 'I ran over to her.'
- Use normal rather than high-blown or old-fashioned language. e.g. 'I proceeded to engage the youthful fellow in conversation.' Instead: 'I spoke to the teenager.' Strunk & White, in *The Elements of Style* (a must-read), urge their readers to avoid 'the elaborate, the pretentious, the coy, the cute'. Good advice.
- Try to use short rather than long words. e.g. 'mobile' NOT 'mobile telephone'; 'pram' NOT 'perambulator'. These days, with texting and e-mailing, we tend to naturally use shorter words, and abbreviations. Just try to use the most appropriate words to the piece you are writing.
- Speak in the concrete rather than the abstract. Be specific! e.g. 'His life was filled with sadness.' BETTER: 'He was sad because he was the only one left of his family.'

BEWARE THE THREE 'A'S': ADJECTIVES, ADVERBS & ABSTRACT NOUNS

These are often called the 'banana skin' parts of speech because when there are too many of them, the reader starts to slip and slide all over the page and eventually off it, never to return.

The three A's clog up your prose, making it unwieldy and cluttered. Of course you are allowed to use all three, otherwise why would they exist? Just do it with care; moderation is the key with these banana skins.

QUALIFIERS

Qualifiers: these change the meaning of other words e.g. quite, very, pretty etc. Strunk & White say that qualifiers 'are the leeches that infest the pond of prose, sucking the blood of words'. So now you know!

Example: 'Martin is quite a nice little chap.' Is he nice or not? Is he really little? You must decide and describe him accurately.

CLICHÉS

Oh, I could talk for a long time about clichés. Clichés are second-hand, well worn phrases and they are too easy to use. Clichés are for lazy writers and you're not lazy, are you? The ones you know include these classics: 'heart of gold', 'as light as a feather', 'green with envy'. My best recommendation is that you cut their tiny hearts out, making them the 'little dead places' that David Long says they are.

However, they can be used in dialogue (remember people speak in clichés), but try not to overuse them. As a rule, try always to write fiction in an original way—it will keep your writing fresh.

IMAGERY

Imagery is mental pictures or figures of speech, like similes and metaphors; they paint vivid pictures for the reader and make her understand exactly what you mean. Using imagery can inject freshness and beauty into your short fiction. It is all about visualising. The word imagery comes from 'imagine'; we all imagine in different ways. Use that.

SIMILE

A simile is an expression including the words 'like' or 'as' to compare one thing with another. e.g. 'Ciara is like a stone.'

METAPHOR

A metaphor is a 'short' simile, beloved of poets especially. It's when you compare a person or object to something that is thought to have similar characteristics. 'Ciara is a stone.'

In a poem, Carol Ann Duffy refers to falling in love as 'glamorous hell'. Sometimes writing invokes the same sort of feeling in writers: we are compelled to write and, when it is going well, we love it, but when it goes badly it can be a sort of hell.

However, if you keep writing and reading through the hellish periods, you *will* produce good, publishable work. So write, write, write and read, read, read, and all will be well. I promise.

 ## FAVOURITE SHORT STORIES

'The Pale Gold of Alaska' by Éilís Ní Dhuibhne from *The Pale Gold of Alaska* (Headline Review, 2001).
'A Paris Story' by David Constantine from *Under the Dam* (Comma Press, 2005).

'The Isabel Fish' by Julie Orringer from *How to Breathe Underwater* (Viking, 2004).

'Babette's Feast' by Isak Dinesen from *Anecdotes of Destiny* (Penguin Classics, new ed., 2001).

'Extra' by Yiyun Li from *A Thousand Years of Good Prayers* (Harper Perennial, 2006)

 REFERENCE BOOKS

Strunk and White, *Elements of Style* (Longman, 1999)

Heffron, Jack: *The Writer's Idea Book* (Writer's Digest Books, 2002)

 IDEAS FOR FURTHER EXPLORATION

ONE

Write a 100 word piece describing what it's like for a character to be beside the sea/shoreline. Use your senses. What does s/he see, hear, smell, touch, taste? How does s/he feel by the sea? Avoid clichés, hackneyed phrases etc.

When you're done, read an Alasdair McLeod story, and an extract from Hemingway's *The Old Man and the Sea*, to examine their approach to writing about the sea.

TWO

Finish these sentences using unusual images. No clichés allowed —nothing we've heard before!

Marty's cat was as scruffy as . . .

The child ran towards me; his face was as . . .

The rain fell like . . .

Mona was childish, it always seemed like she . . .

The house reminded me of home. It had . . .

His skin was as red as . . .

The bread she made was horrible; it tasted like . . .

Pádraig looked like his mother. He . . .

Lena's hair was as . . .

The snake fizzed across the ground towards me; its body had . . .

His skin was as pale as . . .

The cake was delicious; it was as . . .

Our view was terrible. It looked like . . .

CHIKA UNIGWE

SETTING

'One (villa) is set high on a cliff....and overlooks the lake ... Supported by rock, as if by the stilt-like shoes of the actors in (a) tragedy ... It enjoys a broad view of the lake which the ridge on which it stands divides in two ... From its spacious terrace, the descent to the lake is gentle ...'

This quotation (taken from a brochure) is attributed to Pliny the Younger, describing one of his two villas in Bellagio. I was recently a fellow at the Bellagio Institute in Italy and I was fortunate enough to have stayed at the villa built on the spot Pliny was probably describing. His description is so vivid and well-observed that even the familiar gives me pleasure. Although this extract is not taken from a work of fiction, it is, nevertheless, a good example of what setting is and how setting can function in any given work, so much so that I believe it is a good place to start writing this topic from.

So what is setting? What is included in that very broad term? Simply put, setting is not just the time and place of a story, but also the mental landscape of the characters who inhabit a particular narrative. It is therefore often linked to mood or meaning. It is also by its very nature interconnected with description. Setting helps us understand themes and characters better in a narrative. If I may draw on a culinary analogy and liken fiction to food which still needs to be cooked, setting is then the fire with which to cook it. It is the soul of any work. It is often advisable to introduce setting as early as possible in a narrative. A good example is the opening of Mary Watson's short story, 'House Call':

> The glass door to number fifteen was frosted and this chilled Sean whenever he inserted the key in his own lock. His door faced number fifteen in a bare brick-and-cement block of flats. Each time he stood before his door, his back to the mountain, he felt his skin prickle with goose-pimples.

In one of my favourite novels, *The God of Small Things*, Arundhati Roy begins the novel by placing her story in a geographical place and time and drops her readers right into the physical landscape of her narrative. We see Ayenemem. We know what month of the year it is. We feel the rain on our faces:

> May in Ayemenem is a hot brooding month. The days are long and humid. The river shrinks and black crows gorge on bright mangoes in still dustgreen trees. Red bananas ripen. Jackfruits burst. Dissolute bluebottles hum vacuously in the fruity air. Then they stun themselves against clear windowpanes and die, fatly baffled in the sun.

Every single line of the opening paragraph paints an incredibly meticulously observed picture. We know exactly where we are. We can see it. We can feel it. We know what time of year it is. What the weather is like. And we know that the story that follows is not likely to be a feel good story. And indeed it is not.

The opening paragraphs of both Roy's novel and Watson's short story show the power of a keen sense of observation. They link the physical landscape to the mental landscape of the characters. They also assure the readers that they are in the hands of skilled guides. Perhaps particularly in the *The God of Small Things*. We trust the writer that she knows enough of Ayemenem and of its monsoon that we are willing to place ourselves in her hands and lose ourselves in the story. We do not for a moment, doubt her credibility. This brings me to my second point.

Research. Research. Research. If your story is set in a physical location you are not familiar with, please spend some time and do some research. If it is impossible to go there, ask people who have been. Use the internet. Use the library. There is nothing as jarring to readers as reading a story and having trouble with its verisimilitude. When I started work on my novel, *On Black Sisters' Street*, a novel which tells the story of Nigerian commercial sex workers in Antwerp, I went to the red light district of Antwerp and walked the streets. I entered cafés. I listened and spoke to Nigerian women who were in the same business as my characters. I soaked in the atmosphere of the street at night. I listened to its voice. I watched. I took down notes. So when I sat down to write I had an aid to help me recreate the setting. And I believe that my writing is the better for it. If you are using a well known location, do not overlook the obvious. I—like so many others I know—enjoy the thrill of being shown the familiar. If your location is imagined, know it as well as you do the back of your hand.

You have to be convinced of the truth of its imagined reality. If it is not real to you, it will be impossible for you to convince a reader of its reality either. In 'Leng Lui is for Pretty Lady', the opening story in *One World: A Global Anthology of Short Stories*, Elaine Chiew aptly captures the Hong Kong of its immigrant domestic workers. One particularly moving scene is when the protagonist of her story, Alina, ends up unfairly in jail:

> Spend one night in a Hong Kong cell, the walls are cement cinderblocks without windows, and the bars remind me of the cages Abuela kept her prized roosters in. I sleep on a cold cement bench, and there's no blanket. Deep in the night, my heart aches to hold my little girl, and I cry out to José. But he cannot hear me now. I sing softly to myself, ballads my Abuela taught me when I was little, and the sound of my own voice makes me scared.

A reader comes out of the story feeling that she has been there. However, while the importance of setting cannot be over-emphasised, it is vital to remember not to overload the reader with too many details as this can become boring and therefore counter-productive. Many readers tend to switch off when they are presented with long and windy descriptions of say, time and space. There is the urge to shout, enough already! When I read narratives where the writer takes me on a tiring journey through a landscape, it is like being constipated on too much food. It becomes impossible to enjoy the food any longer, no matter how tasty it is. A skilled writer breaks up the setting in bits and inserts them in manageable doses throughout the story. Continuing with the culinary analogy, a writer is like a cook with a kitchen full of different pots of spices. If he uses all the spices at once, he ruins a good dish. The secret is in the amount of spices added and at what stage of the cooking they are added. This is what distinguishes a poor cook from a good one. A skilled writer knows that it is sometimes enough to give the reader a general idea of where the story is set and then gradually zoom in like a camera lens into particular locations. Damon Galgut's short story, 'The Lover', is a good example of how to do this. He opens with:

> No particular intention brings him to Zimbabwe, all those years ago. He simply decides one morning to leave and get on a bus that same night. He has it in mind to travel around for two weeks and then go back.

And then bit by bit he strips the geographical space of its generality and exposes particular places:

> He takes the overnight train to Victoria Falls. He lies in his bunk, hearing the breathing of strangers stacked above and below him, and through the window sees villages and sidings flow in and out of the dark, the outlines of people and cattle and leaves stamped out in silhouette against the lonely night, then flowing backward again, out of sight into the past

We go from Zimbabwe, the country, to Victoria Falls and then to the interior of a train. What we see and hear and feel, in the example above, we do through the eyes of the protagonist. This is a technique some writers use to expose setting. I have often found that I enjoy being shown the setting through the eyes of a character rather than narration.

Another common way of revealing both mental and physical landscapes is through dialogue. Have your characters talk about the weather, the taste of food, the time of day. In Ngugi's short story, 'Minutes of Glory', we follow one of the characters, Beatrice, as she knocks on a door:

'Who is that?'
'It's me. Please open'
'Who?'
'Beatrice'
'At this hour of the night?'
'Please.'

Without having to tell the readers what time of the night it is, we infer through the short exchange that it is very late, certainly not the time of day for paying social visits. We can not only visualize the darkness, but we also have an idea of the state of mind of Beatrice and the sort of relationship between her and the person whom she has gone to see.

Apart from creating both a physical and mental atmosphere for a narrative, setting is also used to advance plot and in some cases, heighten tension. A writer writing about the deteriorating relationship between a mother and a daughter could have both of them stuck inside a room during a riot that lasts for several days. Neither can escape the other. How do they handle this? How does their already fragile relationship deal with this? In both extracts from Galgut and Ngugi, the setting becomes a reflection of the characters' inner state. Does your character have an attachment to the house you have just sketched? Is it of some emotional importance? Exploit this and use setting to give your character depth. Use it to advance the plot of your narrative.

Furthermore, setting is not only useful for advancing plot and heightening tension, it is also bound to have an influence on how characters act or speak. For example, a teenager in a story set in eighteenth century Lagos City is bound to talk, if not act differently from a youth in the same city in the twenty first century. To get the setting right, you not only need to create a physical space that rings true to the world you are creating but a language that does as well. Characters in narratives ought to be a reflection of the worlds that they inhabit. A conscientious writer is always aware of that.

Now that we know what setting is, and we know its usefulness, what are the ways in which a writer could develop setting in a narrative? As mentioned at the start of this essay, it is pertinent to know the physical location of the narrative as well as you know the back of your hand. It is also useful to know the time the narrative occurs. Knowing the time and place will help you structure your characters to act appropriately. A character in a story set in Paris in the winter might look out of her hotel room to see a field of snow. But not so a woman in tropical Nigeria.

Show the world the characters live in. I remember taking part in a writing workshop several years ago and presenting a short story I was very proud of for peer critiquing. A more experienced writer in the group told me that while the premise of my story was interesting, its major drawback was the lack of multi-dimensionality in its characters. He said he wondered about the shoes my protagonist would wear. What sort of shoes were they? Would he polish them? His obsession with my protagonist's shoes led to a much more rounded, believable story at the end of the workshop. My characters lived.

In showing the world of your narrative, resist the urge to explain. It is more rewarding to opt for suggestion rather than explanation. Give your readers the joy of figuring out things for themselves rather than spoon-feeding them. Good writers immerse readers in narratives which include all the senses. For instance, rather than writing, 'The day was hot and dry', consider this extract from 'The Last Trip' by Sefi Atta:

> Her son, Dara, is asleep on the mattress, face up. He rubs the eczema patches around his eyes and wheezes. A miniature oscillating fan blows dust over him. She has considered leaving her windows open to give him some relief. The heat indoors is unbearable, but the air in this part of Lagos has a sour taste.

How much more pleasant is the reading experience for being shown rather than being told what the weather was like.

Finally, in a reverse of the normal order of things, I would like to end by sharing with you one of the most useful things I have learnt about the craft of writing fiction, which is to create a setting for my narratives before I even start writing. I do not always use all the details I have put down but then I have a regular well to draw from while I write. This also helps to make setting as alive and as memorable as possible. I do not know many writers who enjoy taking the time to create setting. It certainly is not one of my favourite things to do when I am itching to let go and write. But the energy it requires is rewarded manyfold in the result it gives. One can simply not ignore this if one is dedicated to writing good quality fiction. And that surely is our shared goal as writers.

REFERENCE BOOKS

One World: A Global Anthology of Short Stories (New Internationlist, 2009)

Atta, Sefi: *LAWLESS and Other Stories* (Farafina, 2007)

Galgut, Damon: 'The Lover', *The Paris Review* (24 February, 2009)

Roy, Arundhati: *The God of Small Things* (Harper Perennial, 1998)

Unigwe, Chika: *On Black Sisters' Street* (Jonathan Cape, 2009)

Wa Thiongo, Ngugi: 'Minutes of Glory', from *The Art of the Story: An International Anthology of Contemporary Short Stories*, Ed. Daniel Halpern. (Penguin Group, 1999)

Watson, Mary: *Moss* (Kwela Press, 2004)

 IDEAS FOR FURTHER EXPLORATION

Here are a few ideas to help you practice setting. They are designed to work together but can also be done independently of each other.

ONE

- Choose a room in your house as the setting for this exercise
- Imagine you are seeing this room for the first time
- On a sheet of paper, write down everything you can see in the room
- Repeat for smell and touch
- In one word, write down the sort of mood you want the room to evoke in a reader

- Carefully choose and discard the details you need/do not need to evoke the particular feeling
- Write an opening scene for a short story

TWO

- Pick a face out of a magazine
- Give it a name
- Create a back-story for him/her: background, age, hobbies, idiosyncrasies, etc.
- Place this character in the room you've chosen for Exercise One (skip this if you have not done the previous exercise)
- Write a paragraph on a day in this character's life without using any adjectives

THREE

- Introduce another character
- Through dialogue show this character's relationship to the character in the previous exercise
- Reveal through dialogue the character in Exercise Two, ensuring that his mental landscape imitates that of the room he is in.
- Challenge yourself to finish the story in 2,500 words.

ALEX KEEGAN

24: THE IMPORTANCE OF THEME

L ast night, with my son, I watched the last two episodes of the show 24 — a violent, technology-rich, twist-and-turn thriller, that makes 'complex plotting' a serious understatement. That is twenty-four HOURS of film.

I woke this morning to realise how little of the plot-line has stayed with me, but how two things had. The first things I remember are the small islands of humanity in the long story. That is, despite all the 'bells and whistles', it's all about *character*.

The second thing is, despite countless gun-battles, murders, subterfuge, agents and double-agents, despite secret organisations, kidnapped presidents, and bio-terrorism, what the whole 24 hours boiled down to was one essential thing: whether or not it is imperative to stay within the law, or whether, if we step outside the law for family, for honour, to save a loved one, for moral justice, for revenge for a loved one, and inflict violence if it is 'the only way' to save many, is it ever right or excusable?

This question is core. It is the glue which holds together the whole, or the current the film sails on.

The film opens with the hero Jack Bower on trial for acting as Jack Bower has always done, violently, outside the law, to stop terrorism. His parent organisation has been disbanded and now 'squeaky-clean' society has him over the coals. Over many series fans of Jack Bower have lived with his set of beliefs, accepted them as 'the only way'. Now their hero is being unjustly taken to task. Jack knows how many would have died had he not done what he felt he had to do. We, the viewers feel the same.

Jack is not contrite. It looks like the end of Jack. The cross-examination is clever, because while we 'believe in Jack' and understand him, we begin to understand the personal cost he has faced. Somewhere he says that it's not about the law, not about right or wrong, it's about finding a way to do your job that you can live with.

As will always happen in 24, a monstrous conspiracy lurks and Jack is suddenly on the run, unable to explain to those who hunt him just what is going on, unseen. He behaves 'badly' in the eyes of his hunters, commits illegal acts and appears to have committed worse, including murder.

On the one side we have the established hero, hunted. On the other side is the (over-keen?) FBI trying to catch him, and much of their conversation is 'moral'.

In the story, one sub-plot concerns a man prepared to cause deaths to find and kill the man who killed his wife. In another, a man has to commit a terrorist act to save his brother's life. In another, an utterly faithful, prepared-to-die bodyguard has to face the unthinkable and investigate the person he protects. In another, the president's daughter pays for her brother's killer to be killed. Later, her mother, (the President of the United States) has to choose between her family and 'doing the right thing'. In another sub-plot Bower is infected by a biological agent and will not allow his daughter to give bone-marrow in the small hope he might live.

There are other similar arguments and counter-arguments, and a few 'set-speeches' about the balance always needing to be struck when fighting evil or choosing between a loved one and one's country. The writers skilfully 'play' the audience and first have them leaning towards one side, then the other.

Throughout the film, family, blood-ties, religion, brotherhood are weighed against the law and 'correct' behaviour. The story's moral stance is to stand on the middle of a see-saw and manipulate it.

THEME

Theme (capital T) (sometimes called premise) is NOT about a story's plot. It's what a story 'says'. It's what a story tells us. It's what a story explains to us about the world, or forces us to consider. Theme is a story's meaning. If we boil down that plot, what is left? How are we altered by reading a story or watching a film?

Does the intricacy of the plot of *One Flew Over the Cuckoo's Nest* *really* matter? Or is what we actually take away the complex humanity of McMurphy, the sanity of those labelled 'insane', McMurphy's journey and that of the Big Indian, and the inhumanity of the mental health system? The book and film are 'saying something'. That is Theme.

Theme is not mere content. 'War' is not a theme. 'Jealousy' is not a theme. A story might show us that in war heroes die and cowards survive but are dead inside. Or a story might show us that we do not know what real bravery is. A story might teach us that jealousy kills, or it might show us that a lack of jealousy is unnatural and leads to victimhood.

Good stories, whether straightforward or complex, take us from one state of knowledge and opinion, to a new state of knowledge and opinion. *Twelve Angry Men* shows us how fact is not fact, how men are blind, how bigotry and our personal histories blind us. A good book or a good film leaves us thinking, something moves in us and we are disturbed by a new awareness. That new awareness was delivered by the story's Theme.

Understanding Theme is like learning to ride a bike. It seems big and frightening and you just don't get it. Then you do and doing what you do, writing for a reason or cycling to the shops, seems so *natural* and the reasons so *obvious* that you cannot understand where the problem was.

When I teach, I operate the 'So What? Test', to discover the underlying Theme of a story.

Let's say a writer describes his story. Think of the story of *One Flew Over the Cuckoo's Nest* as an example. (There is a good synopsis on Wikipedia, if you do not know it, here: *http://en.wikipedia.org/wiki/One_Flew_Over_the_Cuckoo%27s_Nest_(film)*

The discussion might go something like this:

Writer: Well there's this really wild guy who likes to drink and get into fights. He ends up briefly committed to a mental hospital and is a total pain in the ass, winding up the head nurse and generally causing mayhem. I think that'd be very funny.

So What?

What do you mean, 'So What?' Just think of all the funny scenes with this SANE guy, in among all these whack-jobs.

So What?

Huh? Well it would maybe show he's got a good side (still funny of course . . .)

So What?

Um, and maybe, because he's sane, but a bit different, he could show up the Nurse as a bitch.

So What?

Oh I dunno. She isn't going to like it, this sane upstart messing with the way the place is run. Look, the whackos aren't taking their meds because McMurphy doesn't.

So What?

Well this Head Nurse (I called her Ratchet) she's gonna be pretty pissed.

So What? Good name by the way.

Well, she could turn on McMurphy big-time, drug him up or even give him electro-convulsive therapy or something.

So What?

Well, what if it messed McMurphy's brain up?

So What if she did?

Well that shows Ratchet and the system up, doesn't it? There's all these guys, we see them as whackos and so does McMurphy, but he's *getting through to them* and they start to seem human again. The Head Nurse doesn't like that, does she? McMurphy is a danger to her, everything she stands for, how she lives her life.

And?

Well they don't really CARE do they? It's more a case of control, of corralling these guys. McMurphy threatens everything she stands for. She's Head Honcho in a nasty system of oppression and suppression. McMurphy represents hope. He has to be stopped.

And?

Well either he manages to get out and get all his sick friends out (hard to imagine) or they 'get' him, somehow. Either way it makes me think who is sick, really.

So it's not *about* 'funny'?

No.

So it's not *really* 'about' McMurphy?

No, he's just the person who exposes the institution for what it is.

And Nurse Ratchet?

Well, she sort of IS the institution. She represents it.

OK, so what is this story about? What does it say?

It says, the mental health system is corrupt. It's about oppression and suppression and not about succour or cures. McMurphy, though wild and uncontrollable (i.e. he's a bit extreme) exposes this, and for that he must be controlled and oppressed in turn. I think I'm arguing two things, what is madness and what is freedom, and the fact that the mental health care system is oppressive.

So, could you sum that up in a line?

OK: The mental health system is self-serving and oppressive. To challenge it from within leads to death.

COMMON ERRORS IN THEME

In the above description you could be excused for thinking that there is more than one Theme here. There is not. It's merely, as expressed, a sub-theme has been expressed as if it's an equal partner.

It's a common error in beginner and intermediate stories for the writer to have one strong unifying theme and commit the sin of introducing 'evidence' that weakens the theme. That is like arguing a case in court and deliberately undermining your own argument.

In *One Flew Over The Cuckoo's Nest*, a 'good' nurse would be a dangerous element. A good nurse would seriously undermine the idea that ALL the mental health system (or this hospital) was bad. So could you have a good nurse? Sure, but he or she must be destroyed or made to conform. Otherwise your theme becomes diluted into, '*Part* of the mental health system is corrupt.' How wishy-washy is that?

A second error is where the writer introduces 'something he wants to say' which is themed in itself but does not relate to his main theme. If we were to introduce, 'Art is undervalued in modern society' into *One Flew Over*, it would weaken the story.

A story, especially a short story, is saying something, *one* thing about the world. It is a poem to the idea. It sings its proof. It may be subtle and sneak a hand around your ribs and grab the heart or it may hit you in the face with a shovel, but it is, or should be, trying to alter your way of seeing the world.

IS THIS TOO DELIBERATE? IS THIS COOKIE-CUTTING?

Answer. No!

Flannery O'Connor once argued that she wrote to discover what she meant. When asked 'what is the story's theme?' she would answer, 'read the story'.

Frankly, in the first case, I take great issue with her statement. A good short story is a subtle argument. It makes a case by delivering anecdotal evidence. The idea that I would write about, say, rape *to discover my opinion on rape* is patently absurd. It may be the case that we approach a subject by writing in that area, and we *feel* we discover our thoughts, but are we ever surprised by what we think? No! We don't finish an argument or complete a story and think, 'Oh, I never knew I thought that!' Poppycock.

We do, however, sometimes *clarify* our thoughts, or learn to articulate them more clearly, or find certain subtleties in our thoughts, but I resolutely do not believe we did not know beforehand.

When O'Connor said to know her theme you should read her story, that's a clever trick, in my opinion. It's a get-out clause. It's a way of ducking the question. It reminds me of Billy Collins' clever little poem 'Introduction to Poetry' where he says, 'I say drop a mouse into a poem and watch him probe his way out'.

I do understand that merely being told a theme is not the way. I know we must immerse ourselves in a story or a poem and feel it, find it. But that does not mean that, most of the time we cannot state the theme or say, 'this is why I wrote this'.

But, *having a purpose* can sit alongside a feeling of vagueness and not be fully delineated. In fact, that's how I write, myself. And yet how can I write purposefully and not be deliberate, prescriptive, or plotting? How can I end up with a strong theme without 'theming'?

The answer is surprisingly simple. Character.

James Frey in *How to Write a Damn Good Novel* once wrote that Character + Problem + Method of Resolution gives us Theme (he calls it Premise.) Two different characters with the same problem will find different solutions. HOW they do things says something about the world 'as shown by their behaviour'.

Imagine different men discovering their respective wives in bed with another man. Their behaviour largely depends on their character, and how they react 'says something' (in that small world of this story) about the world.

The first man might kill his wife.

Another man might kill the lover.

A third man might kill both.

A fourth man might kill himself.

A fifth man might stop and ask, 'What did I do to make my wife fail?'

A sixth man might not care.

Each reaction says a different thing. Here, the reaction is not dependent on the event, *but on the character exposed to that event.*

Plotters plot, but there is no reason for us to actively drive theme. All we need to do is choose the right character and voice, and begin our story *in media res*. If we are faithful to our characters we can allow them to do 'whatever they choose' knowing the story will go the right way.

If we wish to explore vengeance we must have a character who is vengeful or can be made vengeful, but there is no need to push. We simply choose a character with feelings of the right kind, expose him to a situation and then empathise with him and record his actions. When I write, I often say, 'I don't know where I'm going' yet I almost never stall, never need to think. I surrender to my characters.

Perhaps if I outline a writing exercise I run, the point is made clearer.

GOING BACK TO THE SALOON

Imagine a male character in film, let's begin with an icon, John Wayne. Wayne, especially in the first half of his career, embodied a basic male-American ideal. I won't even articulate that ideal.

Now a character played by John Wayne goes to a bar, whether in 60's New York or some saloon in the Wild West. He is humiliated by one or more guys in the bar and leaves, beaten perhaps, his tail between his legs. If a woman is involved he has lost respect in her eyes.

The story continues and he resolves to return to the bar to face the man or men who humiliated him. Today he goes back to the bar.

Now remember, this is John Wayne circa 1940-1965. He's *a good guy*. In those days, in those films he embodied various American ethics: a man's gotta do what a man's gotta do; fist-fights are manly and kinda fun; if it comes to it, a gun is good etc.

Wayne didn't fight dirty back then. The bad guys did. Wayne would prefer a fist-fight, something 'honourable' but of course, the bad guys would eventually fight dirty, or pull a gun and would pay the price. Wayne would win, *but honourably.*

I ask students to write a short script for the scene. With John Wayne as 'the guy'.

Now flip forward to 1980, Al Pacino for example. Would Al Pacino be quite so concerned with fighting fair or would *his* morality be solely about winning, about revenge? Woody Allen. What would you expect him to do?

Now look at the scripts. With these different characters playing 'the guy', characters who embody different values, the scene changes, doesn't it? The point is, the basic character (embodied in a film-star) often directs how a scene will pan out. The character *contains* the mode of response, and it is the mode of response that gives us Theme. Change the star, change the result!

Wayne would embody 'A man's gotta do what a man's gotta do, but he ALSO embodied, 'with honour.' Pacino might embody, 'Do whatever is necessary, but get even.' In this case the honour or otherwise of the actual fight is irrelevant.

This is the key to writing well and with strong themes. Be cruel to your characters, place them in difficult, testing situations, *but then, do not interfere, trust them to act as they would, let them live.*

So, coming back to me, the writer, I know my beliefs on rape. Unlike O'Connor I would not need to write about rape to discover what I think. But I might wish to explore the edges of this subject, those areas where consent is vague, where one person is not on the same page as the other. To do so I must pick my character or characters with care.

If I chose a crazy, homicidal rapist, I would learn nothing. If I chose a person without sexual drives I would learn nothing. I have to choose a man, a man who might echo me, who thinks he knows what is rape and what isn't and I would put that man into those areas of grey.

I do not need to plot. I do not need to plan. I do not need speeches and carefully placed metaphors. I just live the story, go to the right places, allow my 'ordinary man' to be exposed to the waves, and record what he does. What he does will contain meaning. What he does, what he feels, is what the story means.

In order for our stories to be rich and resonant, they need Theme. They need to *matter,* to 'say something' to give us insight into what it is to be human, and hopefully not in a trite, trivial, soap opera or clichéd way.

That means we need characters who we expect to behave in a certain general (but not specific) way: the racist, the embittered, the deluded, the Walter Mitty, the misogynist, the exploiter, the abuser, the closeted, the downtrodden spouse, the easily-led.

Rather than impose, directly, our morals or opinions on the reader, we simply place the right kinds of characters in situations which will expose them to pressure. Then, by allowing them to respond to their situation we will see truly human problem-solving, and, as Frey said, how they respond contains meaning, Theme Capital T.

 REFERENCE BOOKS

Frey, James: *How to Write a Damn Good Novel* (St Martin's Press, 1987)

 FAVOURITE SHORT STORIES

Saul Bellow, 'A Silver Dish', from *Best American Short Stories of the Century*, Ed: John Updike (Houghton Mifflin, 2000)

Nathan Englander, 'The Twenty-Seventh Man', from *For the Relief of Unbearable Urges* (Vintage, 2000)

Lawrence Sargeant Hall, 'The Ledge', from *Best American Short Stories of the Century*, Ed: John Updike (Houghton Mifflin, 2000)

Ernest Hemingway, 'The Short Happy Life of Francis Macomber', from *The Complete Short Stories of Ernest Hemingway* (Scribner, 1998)

Nathan Englander, 'Tumblers', from *For the Relief of Unbearable Urges* (Vintage, 2000)

Raymond Carver, 'A Small Good Thing', from *Best American Short Stories of the Century*, Ed: John Updike (Houghton Mifflin, 2000)

Raymond Carver, 'Cathedral', from *Cathedral* (Vintage, 1989)

Tim O'Brien, 'The Things They Carried', from *Best American Short Stories of the Century*, Ed: John Updike (Houghton Mifflin, 2000)

John Updike, 'Gesturing', from *Best American Short Stories of the Century*, Ed: John Updike (Houghton Mifflin, 2000)

Saul Bellow, 'Something to Remember Me By', from *Something to Remember Me By* (Martin Secker & Warburg Ltd., 1992)

Ernest Hemingway 'Hills Like White Elephants', from *The Complete Short Stories of Ernest Hemmingway* (Scribner, 1998)

 IDEAS FOR FURTHER EXPLORATION

One example is the 'Return to the Saloon' exercise in the essay. Here is another:

The meaning of a work is not merely in the semantics, the dictionary meanings of the words, phrases, sentences. It is also tied up in tone, colour, weight and speed of the words. 'I-AM-GOING-TO-TOWN, NOW' hardly has the same meaning as 'I'm off to town, now!'

Writers often have an unintended dissonance between the direct (semantic) meaning of their words and the meaning conveyed by the colour and music of their narrative. Good writing has actuality, musicality (and metaphor, if any) all working together.

Now, imagine a man, perhaps 45, 50 or a little older. He has received a letter or a telegram. The reader does not know what the telegram says. Maybe the telegram tells the man his son has just died in Iraq, maybe it's a telegram saying his suspected cancer is NOT a cancer. Maybe his daughter has been found alive and well after disappearing six months ago. The man might be brilliantly happy, terribly sad and wretched, overwhelmingly proud. Just do not tell me how he feels or mention the content of the message, AT ALL (not even a hint!)

Now the man goes out of his house, or the farmhouse, into the yard, towards the old barn . . . What does he see? HOW does he see it?

If we the narrators describe what he sees, without at any time mentioning the contents of the letter or his mood, the reader should have a feeling, an overall joy, or sadness, or pride, or fear.

There is the 'pathetic fallacy' that the weather 'finds us out' that if we are down it will rain on us. The idea here is, solely from what the middle-aged man sees and how he sees it, we should sense his mood and believe-in-advance the content of the letter. If we write how Joe walks out, the sun is bright, the old barn looks pleased to meet him, the new-born lambs are friskily gambolling in the meadow, Jess his sheepdog yips, comes to him and licks his hand, he sees primroses breaking out . . . and the smell of breakfast makes him take a deep, glorious breath . . .

Get the idea?

All you need is an imaginary set of telegrams, and a picture of an old farmyard in your head. As an individual you should read the happiest telegram, then describe Joe walking out into the yard. When that job is done, take a break, then read the saddest, most terrible telegram, then describe Joe walking out into the yard.

The two descriptions should be very different. What we see and how we see it depends on our core mood and our immediate thoughts.

Working in a group, we should be able to guess at which telegram Joe has just read. Remember, the good writer does not cheat. If Joe's son has just been killed and you write, 'Joe stumbled into the filthy yard, tears welling up. Black dust swirled up into his face turning to a deathly cement on his broken-hearted face . . .' you have cheated about 400 times.

LANE ASHFELDT

BUILDING A WORLD

Given the rise in 'how to' theory about storytelling, which can give people the impression they need an MA before they even begin to write, it's useful to compare telling a story with building a house. A complicated job, then. Not one for amateurs? That depends. There is a huge gap between a cave dwelling and the kind of showy glass tower that requires a team of architects and three construction firms to erect. Somewhere in between are some of the loveliest houses ever built—homes that people made up as they went along, using local stones or wood. Homes they learnt to build by watching closely, or by helping out when their neighbours built a house.

When you tell a story, though, you are attempting to build not just a house but a whole imaginary world for your reader. The world of your story may be one that is already familiar to you, it may be one you have pieced together from research, or it may be an imaginary, futuristic or fantastical world. That doesn't matter. What matters is that you believe in this world, and that you can convince your readers to believe in it too.

You need to give enough detail to convince, but not so much that you bore your audience or display inconsistencies. The worst moment for any storyteller (and it is a moment familiar to many of us from our playground days), is when someone in the audience says, 'But you said such and such before, so that can't be true. You're making it up!' So, how much detail is enough? A tough question, and one that has different answers depending on what genre you are working within, who your readers are, and on your own individual writing style.

In historical fiction (and this is also true of science fiction, speculative, and fantasy fiction) writers have above average amounts of information to share with the reader, because they are looking to create an unfamiliar world for the reader to live in. But they must be careful how they go about it. This information is best revealed gradually, as a camera pulls out imperceptibly from close-up to long shot.

One reason why the revelation of detail can be a difficult thing to manage is that, when a writer takes on a research task, like any researcher they can become fascinated by the detail they uncover. Research can be fun to do. Say you decide you want to write a story set in 1930s Argentina, a world you know little about. So, you find out what you need to know by whatever means available. If you have friends or colleagues who can help, you contact them. You may choose to visit a library, you may choose to visit Argentina. Whatever way you approach the task, it gets you away from your routine for a while, and you make lots of notes about Argentina in the 1930s . . .

And then what? Well, here's the annoying bit: you get rid of most of it. You don't throw it away, exactly, but you make it almost invisible. Why? Because when you come to fit that research into your story, unless it has a function in the narrative, it may hold things up. Writers of highly plot-driven fiction will find the rule of thumb is, if it doesn't advance the plot, cut it out. Writers of historical or literary fiction may have a certain amount of leeway, but still, the more time spend describing the lovely 1930s dress your heroine wore, and the car-free 1930s road she was walking down, the less time you will spend on your main job, which is to tell the story.

QUESTIONS THE READER WANTS ANSWERED

Who is the girl in the lovely dress?
What is going on?
When is this happening?
Where is she?
Why is she walking down this particular road?

Who, what, when, where and why are the classic questions a journalist expects to find answered on a single-page press release. But these questions are relevant to a short story too. A good short story contains no wasted space.

Some stories last only a single page, others take up five, ten, maybe thirty pages. A page is a sizable dent in any of them. By about a hundred words in, a short story writer must convince their reader there is something going on in this world they're building, something that the reader urgently needs to know about. If they fail, the reader will disappear inside another world, read a different story.

So, the trick is to lure the reader into the world of the particular story you want to tell. And how does a writer learn this trick?

Like many writers, I learnt to write fiction by reading, writing, and making mistakes. On a personal level, I don't get along too well with instruction manuals: if there's a way to go wrong with heating a ready meal or assembling an item of flat-packed furniture, I will find it. Stuff I have learnt by trial and error, on the other hand, the way my granny taught me to bake a cake, I can remember. (I ought to add that she was not the kind of granny who used recipes, she was the kind who used whatever was handy, so baking with her was never a boring, by-numbers kind of thing, it was a sort of investigation of what was in the cupboard and how those ingredients might usefully be thrown together to make something tasty.)

While I don't believe there's such a thing as an infallible recipe or manual for building a story, writing and editing techniques can be learned. And applying them can help take a rough draft forward. In the following pages are two extracts: one from an early draft of 'Dancing on Canvey', a piece I wrote which entailed a fair bit of research, and one from the story as it was eventually published.

This was the first short story I wrote based on a historical event, and I made the classic beginner's error of becoming overly involved in research. I read all I could find on the subject, a flood on the east coast of Britain in 1953. I visited a newspaper library, and was daunted by the regulars (presumably historians) who were hard at work in the best desks by the time I had struggled to fill in my pink slips. My newspapers were delayed because of an error I'd made on the request slips, and when they finally arrived I was childishly pleased to find that they were not on microfiche but a wooden stick. The wait was worthwhile; some useful facts emerged, and, combined with a visit to Canvey, this helped me to feel confident both on facts and on physical detail.

Travel to the location of your story is a luxury that, though enjoyable, is not always necessary. I have written other research-intensive stories, such as 'Off the Map', without visiting the places used as settings. Obviously all this research made me confident that I knew the background to this story, but it took time.

Your own research will naturally depend on your own interests. It may be about football or calligraphy or epidemiology. It may take in visits to workplaces or libraries or parish archives, it could involve following current or predicted future trends in science, medicine or fashion. Whatever it is, it will be tailored to match your budget and available time, and be conducted online or offline according to preference and practicality.

So, having gathered all this material, how to structure it?

To have done a little less research might have made things easier, I realised, because when it came to it I found it hard to move on. The more obscure the information was, the more I wanted to keep it. So my next mistake was the time I spent exploring all sorts of plot options and narrative changes that might have enabled me to hang on to stuff. Not even important stuff, just stuff that I'd picked up and liked, the way a child collects coins or bits of plastic.

These efforts gave me an insight into the origins of some of the varieties of historical novel out there. Because it seems that if you can assign a piece of information a job in your plot, then you are justified in keeping it. Quest narratives often take an object of historical significance and invest in it some contemporary relevance, so it advances a 'now' plot while also advancing a reader's understanding of historical times. Some writers also mix genres —historical, horror, and crime fiction may all be rolled into one if your modern day Egyptologist discovers an ancient artefact capable of bringing evil zombies to life. And a detective or archaeologist has the perfect excuse to go fact-finding, even to find facts that lead nowhere. This adds dramatic tension too: the zombie from the past is out to get you now, the world needs to be saved, and so on. Another variant is the family saga mixed with the past—an unsuspecting contemporary narrator discovers a skeleton in the cupboard of their personal family history.

Michel Faber is a writer who likes to mix up genres and move from one to another but is perhaps best known for his historical novels 'The Hundred and Ninety-Nine Steps' and 'The Crimson Petal and the White'. On the subject of fiction inspired by the past, Faber has said that 'the problem is, it is not easy to write fiction set in bygone ages without doing all the things that good narrative sense tells us not to'. In his foreword to 'All The King's Horses' (Fish Publishing, 2006), he gently sends up writers who, in an effort to prevent readers from visualising a story via their default setting (the present), feel obliged to continually remind them it is set in the past. 'Those who have carefully studied, eg, 17th century Flemish butchers as 'background research' for their story are often condemned to tell us every little thing they've learned about butchery, the Flemings, and the 17th century in general.'

Both century and theme were different in the case of 'Dancing on Canvey', but the principle was the same, and my first attempts at writing this story suffered from similar faults. After reading around the topic and toying with a few rough drafts, I realised I had enough material for a novel or two. In a novel, this information might have been distributed over multiple narrators or timeframes, or more complex subplots could have been introduced—all options I considered, early on. But I was not writing a novel, and a short story did not afford the same scope. Having some experience as an editor of short fiction, I knew I had to make things simple. I chose to create a fictional narrator, Gwynnie, a young girl in her final year of primary school, and focus on how the flood in her home town affects her, her family, and a boy at school who she is just getting to know. The story's events would be based closely on the actual flood which took place on the evening of Saturday 31 January 1953, with the time-frame restricted to the days immediately before and after it. I had discovered that a dance was held in the town on the evening of the flood, and naturally this helped give a focus to the story, while staying true to real events.

Below is an early draft of the first page. This draft, which was to change radically before the story was sent out, demonstrates some classic mistakes of a first piece of historical fiction. Hysterically historical, you might say.

DANCING ON CANVEY, 1953 (ROUGH DRAFT, 2005, UNPUBLISHED)

Ever since Christmas we've had double art on Friday afternoons, and we have been making what our teacher calls a frieze about our town on a single very long scroll of paper which he says will be displayed in the new memorial hall. Each table has a different section of the scroll of paper and a different topic to explore on it. Yellow Table is making pictures of Viking and Roman remains. Red Table is drawing the thousands of sheep who made their home on Canvey back when it was not one island but five marshy islands that were often flooded in high tides, and is describing the salty cheeses the shepherds made here for trading with London. I am on Green Table: our job is to investigate and illustrate what Mr Frome calls the Dutch invasion.

One of the children on my table asks if this for our 11+ and Mr Frome says no. He adds that it is good for us to practise note-taking and information gathering, for these are skills that will serve us well when we grow up, whatever our occupations.

'Sir, when I turn fifteen I will leave school and be a fisherman like my dad,' Johnny says. 'If they hadn't changed the law I'd leave sooner. All I need to know is how to sail a boat, how to swim and how to catch fish. And, sir, I can't learn none of that at school.'

Mr Frome says that until his fifteenth birthday Johnny must join in with the other children, however much he wants to catch fish. He tells Johnny to sit at the green table for a change; it will be useful for a young man who wants to work with the sea to realise how strong an opponent it can be.

The rough draft presents the following issues that needed to be resolved:

- The piece begins with history, as if that is the story.
- History is trumpeted loudly, and too much of it crammed in.
- Characters and their dialogue seem designed only to reveal further period detail.
- The narrator's voice is unconvincing.
- Indirect speech and summary are used to describe events that could, with a lighter touch, be shown more directly.

Although both first pages reach an identical point in the narrative, the published version is better paced. It's interesting to note that it manages to include an entire short scene which the rough draft lacked.

DANCING ON CANVEY (FROM 'THE FISH ANTHOLOGY', FISH PUBLISHING, 2007)

Friday morning I stagger up the steep grassy bank of the sea wall on Smallgains and walk along the top, creek to my left, road to my right. The odd wave sends spray flying up, and the wind curls between my legs, snapping at the skirt of my school gabardine.

Archie and his friend Jim try to follow me. 'Get down!' I tell them. 'You're not allowed up here.' Nor am I, of course. Strictly speaking.

'I'll tell Mam on you,' Archie yells, and pokes his tongue out at me before running ahead towards school until he's just a small speck down at ground level.

It's weird if you think about it, this island that's not really an island anymore with its tall grassy banks to hold it in place. Even now with the tide not fully in, if the sea were level both sides of the wall it would lap at Archie's shoulders. Maybe his nose, even. Not that you do stop to think of it normally, it's just this thing we've been doing in art has it all fresh in my head.

Double art last class. Everyone fidgets while the teacher hands out half-finished scrolls. Since Christmas we've been making a frieze of the island. Yellow Table has covered theirs with Danish and Roman remains; Red has made a grassland dotted with cotton wool sheep and a cut-out shepherd. I'm on Green Table. Yesterday I sketched the Dutch Cottage with its thatched roof and octagonal base, like a windmill minus the arms. Today I'll colour it in.

When Mr Frome hands out sheets of lined paper and tells us to describe what's happening in our pictures, a girl on Blue Table asks will this come up in our 11+. The answer's no. 'But good handwriting,' Mr Frome says firmly, 'is a skill that will serve you well whatever your future occupation.'

That's when Johnny Deakin starts.

'Soon as I turn fifteen I'll be a fisherman like my dad,' he says. 'Fishermen don't need to read or write, sir. I'd leave school now if I could.'

The sea wall is a better place to begin than the classroom. The new scene introduces the narrator, Gwynnie, as she is walking to school with her brother Archie, and it also introduces the island. The date has dropped from the title, allowing period to be indicated by the wind 'snapping at the skirt of [her] school gabardine'. Some details of the island's past have also been trimmed, providing space for dialogue, and this gives a sense of Gwynnie's personality and of the constraints placed on her by her family. A spat with Archie shows the curious half-child, half-adult position she occupies as one of his carers. So, the new opening foregrounds character and indicates familial tensions, while also hinting at the ominous physical strangeness of the island.

It's worth saying, though, that in redrafting the story I did not apply a rigid checklist of what and what not to do. Not every change in redrafting is planned in detail because when a story is taking shape the writer works fast, making many small changes from one draft to the next. Again, this process makes me think of building. Have you ever observed how a builder assembles his materials ahead of starting a new job, ordering in all the bricks, cement, sand and so on that he needs? Later, once the job is up and running, he may find he lacks a plank of wood; there's a batch of wet cement that will harden if he runs out to the nearest hardware shop to buy wood, so instead he rummages in the skip for a suitable piece of wood. With an air of triumph, he trims it to size and places it where it's needed.

Those moments are magic. They're what makes a job worth doing.

Going back to my story, it is hard to say exactly what spurred me to make this new scene. A decision to open the story on the sea wall would have been entirely logical (it is a crucial location for the story: it is here that Gwynnie realises the island is in danger, it is here that she meets Johnny, it is here that the water breaks through). But it's likely the choice was fuzzier than that. That by the time of redrafting, I had some scraps of writing lying around and chanced on something that was a better fit. What matters is, it worked. As soon as this scene was in place, the story began to stand up independently of me.

I have no wish to waffle mystically about 'inspiration' here. A book on the craft of short story writing should provide more concrete advice than that. But in speaking about their work, other writers report similar experiences. In a piece on research, 'Writing what you come to know', fiction writer and dramatist Derek Neale says: 'Most models of the creative process include an unconscious stage, sometimes called the 'incubation period' where ideas hatch and develop beyond our conscious control.'

Neale cites Kurt Vonnegut: 'You can't really control a piece of fiction [...] Part of the technique is to lose control'.

Without all the messy rummaging for ingredients — without tasting things, trying them out — it is hard for a writer to know which ideas (or scenes, or characters) are the ones to go with, and which to leave aside.

As far as my story went, then, all that remained at this point was to complete it, mindful to avoid the temptation to squeeze in dates, footnotes and other evidence of hard library graft. If all that research had helped me to feel in control of the material, well and good, but this wasn't an essay, and no one would give me any Brownie points for bringing interesting new facts to light. I just had to finish the story. And once it was done, find a publisher for it.

Writers who complete short fiction incorporating research may well find the toughest research assignment of all is to find a publisher. Historical stories tend to be lengthier than their contemporary siblings, and in the UK few publication opportunities exist for longer short stories. Then along came the Fish Short Histories competition for stories of up to that length, and the judges picked 'Dancing on Canvey' as winner.

Perhaps the most useful advice to offer is this: whatever you are writing, whatever world it is that you are looking to build for your reader — do not be afraid to experiment until you find a method, or methods, that work well for you.

REFERENCE WORKS

Ashfeldt, L. 'Dancing on Canvey' in *The Fish Anthology* (Fish Publishing, 2007).

Ashfeldt, L. 'Off the Map' (www.Guardian.co.uk 2006).

Faber, M., foreword to 'All The King's Horses' (Fish Publishing, 2006).

Neale, D., in 'Writing what you come to know': *Creative Writing*, L. Anderson, (ed.), Routledge/The Open University, 2006.

Vonnegut, K., interview published in *The Fiction Magazine*, 1983.

FAVOURITE SHORT STORIES

The following six short stories are more of a current playlist than a greatest hits. They are stories I've read in the past few years that jumped out at me, and that stand up to being read more than once. Anyone who'd like to read them can find them online at Pulp Net: www.pulp.net.

'A Hypothalamus Knight'—Nenad Velickovic
'Brown Sugar'—John Bolland
'Dirty Tickle'—Sara Crowley
'Googlehead'—Alistair Gentry
'Studying to be Clark Kent'—Hazera Forth
'Time Brought to Town in a Big Brown Bag'—Richard Bird

IDEAS FOR FURTHER EXPLORATION

ONE

Take a suitable piece of work you have already, a contemporary story, and set it back in time. For example, think about moving the main events back to the time of WWII, or WWI.

Spend some time researching how your existing setting might have been at that time. How would the events playing out on the stage of war impinged on your setting? Look at the way your characters would have lived then, the normal day-to-day details. Think about people's homes, their work, details about their food, clothing, their fears and worries, hopes and aspirations. (Examples only, the list is endless.) Make lists of details under each heading.

Rewrite your story in whichever era you have chosen.

Then, go back over the story and highlight each 'detail' you have inserted from your lists above. Is each detail strictly necessary? Could you do with less? And conversely, have you enough? It is a fine balance to achieve, as Lane Asfeldt said in her essay.

TWO

Go and mooch round a junk shop, and look for old postcards, old items of paste jewellery, old toys. Sometimes you can find old documents. Medals. Maybe you might see old uniforms, other clothing.

Create the character behind the items. Whose were they? What was the situation in which they might have used them? Use these characters and details as the seeds for stories.

(Thanks to Alison MacLeod for the inspiration behind these exercises).

CATHERINE SMITH

MYTH AND MAGIC: BEYOND 'REALISM' IN THE SHORT STORY

L et's start with some basic definitions. Myth and magic—what are they, and how do they 'work' in short stories?

Myth can be defined as ancient, traditional stories of gods or heroes, often offering explanations of some peculiar fact or phenomenon: why does the sun rise each day and disappear each night? Why is there an echo in a cave? But, as Karen Armstrong points out in her excellent book, *A Short History of Myth,* they're more than just old stories that give naïve explanations of why the world is as it is, and how it came to be so:

> We are meaning-seeking creatures . . . human beings fall very easily into despair, and from the very beginning we invented stories that enabled us to place our lives in a larger setting, that revealed an underlying pattern, and gave us a sense that, against all the depressing and chaotic

evidence to the contrary, life had meaning and value.

Myths also have a moral dimension; they offer not only a fictional 'possibility' they show us the consequences of our actions. Joseph Campbell points out that myth isn't just an arcane system of knowledge — its symbolism goes right to the heart of what it means to be a sentient being. 'Myth,' he claims, '. . . puts you in touch with a plane of reference that goes past your mind and your very being, into your very gut . . . The function of mythological symbols is to give you a sense of "Aha! Yes. I know what it is, it's myself."'

And magic is, according to *Chambers English Dictionary*: 'the art of producing marvellous results by compelling the aid of spirits, or by using the secret forces of nature, such as the power supposed to reside in certain objects as "givers of life": enchantment: art of producing illusions by legerdemain: a secret or mysterious power over the imagination or will.' Magic in fiction tends to appear either in fairy stories or the literary genre known as 'Magical Realism'. Fairy tales are stories of the supernatural, of enchantment, where witches, giants, dragons and dwarves interact with princes, princesses and paupers. Originally transmitted orally, they originate from the twelfth century, but were increasingly incorporated into 'literary' culture from the sixteenth century onwards. In late eighteenth century Germany, the Grimm brothers, Jacob and Wilhelm, gathered forty-nine tales from oral and written sources, and transformed them into 'literary creations'. Between 1812-1852, twelve editions were published; a total of two hundred and ten tales stylised to reflect the 'genuine, folk' tone. Often violent and visceral in content, they weren't really designed for children; the sanitisation of fairy tales occurred later. (For further reading about fairy tales, see

Bruno Bettelheim's *The Uses of Enchantment* and Marina Warner's *From the Beast to the Blonde* — both fascinating, seminal works in this field).

Most of us encountered fairy tales as young children. Once upon a time, we delighted in the possibilities of magic, of worlds beyond our own, of transformation and change, invisibility and reappearance. Mice turned into footmen, pumpkins into golden carriages, frogs into princes. Beasts looked nasty but turned out to be handsome 'underneath'; wolves dressed up as grandmothers, but still had dangerously sharp teeth. Often accompanied by sumptuous illustrations and, if we were lucky, readers who were prepared, in their oral delivery, to cackle like witches or roar like giants, a child's introduction to stories can be, literally, fantastic.

But we don't have to leave these stories behind; they can come with us, all our writing lives.

'Magical Realism' also relies on magic and the supernatural; it's a chiefly literary style or genre originating in Latin America that combines fantastic or dreamlike elements with reality. The term 'magical realism' was first used by the German art critic Frank Roh to describe the unusual realism of primarily American painters such as Ivan Albright, Paul Cadmus, George Tooker and other artists during the 20s. It grew popular in the 20th century with the rise of such writers as Mikhail Bulgakov, Ernst Junger and many Latin American writers, notably Jorge Luis Borges, Gabriel Garcia Marquez and Isabelle Allende. Magical realist stories tend to treat reality as completely fluid and have characters who accept this as normal.

Why do writers use this technique/style/device? It's very liberating, combining elements of the fantastic, magic, fairy stories, science fiction, dream and nightmare. It provides the opportunity to question 'reality' in fiction and poetry, and to question the 'setting' of reality by established, powerful forces. In this sense it can feel like a subversive, thrilling act. It accesses the deep imagination and allows us to tap into our dreams, our nightmares, our fantasies, whilst describing these things without melodrama or hyperbole. It lifts the lid, pushes the envelope. It's a new way of approaching narrative — taking the old certainties of plot development to explore the fantastic.

'Magical Realism' takes the supernatural for granted — characters are subjected to strange and bizarre events, but the background remains stubbornly 'ordinary'. As Julian Birkett notes in *Word Power: A Guide to Creative Writing*, 'The point about magic realism is that the realism is quite as important as the magic. People remember the magic things because they're more unusual, but they take place in a world which is extremely real in the everyday sense. it's the curious relationship between the two, the describing of the extraordinary as though it were the same as ordinary, that gives magic realism its unique effect.'

So how are 'mythical and magical' stories sources of inspiration for writers — and how can we, as fiction writers ourselves, rediscover their potency and rich seams of imagery in our own work? Of course, writers have always used magical and mythical sources for their fiction, either directly or obliquely, both in novels and short stories; there are too many to quote here — please see 'suggested further reading' for more ideas — but let's consider a few examples.

Angela Carter's stunning, lyrical and feminist re-interpretations of traditional fairy stories have long been admired as iconic examples of 'reclaiming' the fairy tale. In re-imagining these stories, she tunes into eternal themes — the conflicts between duty and desire, power and powerlessness. Fairy tales provided her with structures and vehicles for luscious, sensuous descriptions, for ways of re-engaging with traditional 'received' story-telling, always hinting at something sinister beneath the physical surface. In 'Peter and the Wolf', she shows the first encounter between the boy and the wild animals:

> If they had not been the first wolves he had ever seen, the boy would not have inspected them so closely, their plush, grey pelts, of which the hairs were tipped with white, giving them a ghostly look, as if they were on the point of dissolving at the edges; their sprightly, plumey tales; their acute, inquisitive masks.
>
> Then Peter saw that the third wolf was a prodigy, a marvel, a naked one, going on all fours, as they did, but hairless as regards the body although new hair grew around its head.

Carter fuses tradition and imagination with thrilling ease, delighting in the possibilities of the uncanny; her work has inspired many (mostly female) writers to revisit and, frequently, subvert these folk tales for their own fictional ends. Emma Donaghue, in her beguiling, subverting re-interpretations of traditional tales, *Kissing The Witch,* playfully explores relationships between women—familial and sexual. In the opening story of her collection, 'The Tale Of The Shoes', she re-tells the tale of Cinderella with a very different slant:

> Till she came it was all cold.
> Ever since my mother died the feather bed felt hard as a stone floor. Every word that came out of my mouth limped away like a toad. Whatever I put on my back now turned to sackcloth and chafed my skin. I heard a knock-

ing in my skull, and kept running to the door, but there was never anyone there. The days passed like dust brushed from my fingers.

I scrubbed and swept because there was nothing else to do. I raked out the hearth with my fingernails, and scoured the floor until my knees bled. I counted grains of rice and divided brown beans from black.

Nobody made me do the things I did, nobody scolded me, nobody punished me but me. The shrill voices were all inside. Do this, do that, you lazy heap of dirt. They knew every question and answer, the voices in my head. Some days they asked why I was still alive. I listened out for my mother but I couldn't hear her among the clamour.

Magical Realism works wonderfully well in short stories, transporting readers directly into fantastic scenarios whilst providing a seemingly 'comfortable' realism in terms of setting. Of course, it's the discomforting juxtaposition of the 'familiar' with the 'uncanny' that gives this genre its power. As said previously, please see the 'suggested further reading' for ideas, but here's an extract from Peter Carey's short story, 'Do You Love Me?' The characters in this story are anticipating the annual Festival of the Corn, an ancient festival related to the wealth of the earth, where a massive census/inventory of personal possessions, and indeed regions, takes place. The narrator's father is himself a 'cartographer', involved in this consummate list-making. Early on, the narrator records a sense of unease; all is not well; entire regions are rumoured to have disappeared. Increasingly, the certainties of the inventory are undermined:

The next day the I.C.I building disappeared in front of a

crowd of two thousand people. It took two hours. The crowd stood silently as the great steel and glass structure slowly faded before them. The staff who were evacuated looked pale and shaken. The caretaker who was amongst the last to leave looked almost translucent. In the days that followed he made some name for himself as a mystic, claiming that he had been able to see other worlds, layer upon layer, through the fabric of the here and now.

How does all this link into teaching short stories? I've taught creative writing—primarily to adults but also to teenagers and children—for eleven years. Although I'm also a poet, my main passion is short stories; reading them, writing them, encouraging other people to try them. Not unreasonably, most 'How To Teach Creative Writing' guides stress the importance of 'lived experience'—filtered and re-shaped through imagination—that tried and tested adage, 'Write about what you know'. But increasingly, both in my own writing of poetry and prose, and especially since teaching day schools on magical realism in fiction, and running a course for Sussex University entitled 'Myth, Magic and the Imagination' as part of its Certificate in Creative Writing, I've become convinced of the value of re-discovering (or in some cases, encountering for the first time—my own knowledge of Myth is almost entirely self-taught, as 'the Classics' seemed to have fallen out of favour when I was at school) the powerful possibilities of using 'traditional' stories—fairy/folk tales, and myths—as sources of inspiration for writing. It seems to me that these stories are not only part of our cultural inheritance—they've shaped our understanding of what a story is, and what it's for—but also, they're a fantastically rich resource for writers—full of vivid, surreal, otherworldly possibilities; both 'beyond' lived experience but also a way of acknowledging the universality and continuity of story-telling; that stories have the exploration and resolution of conflict at their hearts, and that protagonists are frequently obliged to battle monsters and demons — whether actual or psychological. And it's also interesting to consider, as, most notably, Jung has done, the ways in which mythical archetypes may be dramatic projections, in symbolic images, of the inner life of the psyche.

On the Myth, Magic and the Imagination course, we look mostly at Greek myths (but that's just because it's a short course, and mythology is a huge subject!). We start with Creation myths, move onto metamorphosis/transformation; we descend to Underworlds, explore the meaning and journey of the Hero, become familiar with Heroines, Harpies, Furies, Muses and maligned women in general; engage with archetypes, re-write fairy tales and imagine ourselves to be Sheherazade, conjuring up nightly tales to save her neck. The quality and breadth of student work frequently takes my breath away; Jess Richards, in particular, has engaged with these ideas to produce some stunningly imaginative work, which is already being published and winning prizes in short story competitions. Here's an extract from Jess's own Creation Myth, 'Indigo Runaway', which won first prize in the GRIST International Short Story Competition, organised by the University of Huddersfield:

I run away the day they're going to push up the sky. Everyone's outside making plans. They don't usually want any mention of the sky because it's so low in some places they have to hunch over to walk. All my life it's been this unspeakable thing, this trouble all the adults have. The children and teenagers, like me, we've learnt to collect whispers about it. We've become spies, trading buttons, mirrors, toys, whatever we can find, for secrets.

For weeks the adults haven't talked about anything else; it's like the floodgates have opened. All these words they've kept hidden from us for years are spilling out through the whole community; we're caught in a torrent of words. How terrible it's been for them to live like this. How their world will be transformed once they can walk tall without fear of banging their heads, and the horrific after-effects. I've nearly stopped growing, but I'm still short and haven't hit my head on it yet. They say it feels as if there are a thousand needles which pierce the scalp, the feeling of crashing into it. This lasts for days, and then the blue-white cloud shaped bruises appear across the face. We call them sky tattoos. They take weeks to fade away, longer if they're really deep ones.

My grandfather hit his head on the sky three times in one day and the sky tattoos spread across his head and all over his body. He slept for a month without being able to speak at all, and when he woke up, he could only say words that were all to do with the weather. He rambled endlessly about rain and sunbeams, storms, fog and rainbows, cloud formations. It took months of us listening to him closely to figure out if he'd got any proper thoughts any more, or if he'd just gone simple. They didn't notice I was there, the adults. I sat on the floor in the corner of his room, spying from behind his rocking chair. I wanted to understand what the sky had done to him. His language had changed completely. Rain descriptions, like *squally*, *showers* and *torrential* meant things he didn't want, and the word 'no'. When he was enjoying something, usually thick soup or steamed pudding, he would laugh during spoonfuls and shout joyfully about sunshine, splattering food all over his duvet. Rainbows were used when he was pleased to see someone. He'd get lost in describing the colours in different ways, depending on who he was talking to. Red, he described as boiling point, scalding bathtubs, desire and lust. Green led to descriptions of the temperature required for the germination of seeds, hope and possibility. Blue was ink, loss, persuasion. When he once saw me curled in the corner watching him, he started rambling about indigo runaways. I didn't have a clue what he meant. When he was annoyed or confused he would mutter for hours about cloud formations. *Cumulonimbus, altostratus, cirrus* . . . When he started talking storms, it meant that he'd lost the plot and we all ran for shelter. He'd hurl anything within arms reach. These were the only days he'd leave the house. One day he tore out five fir trees with his bare blue-white hands. I think that's where they got the idea about pushing up the sky from, though everyone is claiming the original plan as their own. He is left with permanent faded sky tattoos all over him, like a wooden table covered in blurred stains from spilled ink.

Jess has also explored imaginative descriptions of 'Personal Hades'—in Stranraer, where she grew up—Lilith and Eve as two contemporary women, one old and one young, mermaid myths, and a story about depression where 'black dogs' are aspects of the three headed Cerberus, who guards the entrance to Hades.

I hope I've whetted your appetite for exploring the magical and mythical and for using these sources as part of your own creative inspiration; a chapter like this can only ever scratch the surface—it can become a lifetime's quest to familiarise yourself with all the rich and vibrant stories, a huge part of our cultural and psychological heritage.

 REFERENCE BOOKS

A Short History of Myth by Karen Armstrong (Canongate, 2006)
The Uses of Enchantment, the Meaning and Importance of Fairy Tales by Bruno Bettelhein (Penguin, 1991)
From the Beast to the Blonde by Marina Warner (Vintage, 1995)
Word Power, a Guide to Creative Writing by Julian Birkett (A&C Black, 1998)
Burning Your Boats: Collected Short Stories by Angela Carter (Vintage Classics 1998)
Kissing the Witch by Emma Donaghue (Harper Teen, 1998)
Collected Stories by Peter Carey (University of Queensland Press, 2001)
The Hero With A Thousand Faces by Campbell, Joseph, (Fontana, 1993)
A Dictionary of Creation Myths by Leeming, D and Leeming, M, (Eds) (OUP, 1994)

 FAVOURITE SHORT STORIES

Most of these are entire anthologies. Enjoy:

The Greek Myths by Robert Graves (QPD, 1991)
Complete Fairy Tales by Brothers Grimm (Routledge, 2002)

Angela Carter, 'The Bloody Chamber' and 'Black Venus' from her
  Collected Short Stories (Vintage Classics, 1998)
Magic for Beginners by Kelly Link (Harper Perennial 2007)
Collected Stories by Gabriel Garcia Marquez (Penguin, 2008)
Reshape Whilst Damp, The Asham Prizewinners' Anthology, Ed:
  Carole Buchan (Serpent's Tail, 2000)
Fictions by J Borges (Penguin 2000),
The Aleph and Other Stories by J Borges (Penguin, 2004)
Fragile Things by Neil Gaiman (Headline Review, 2007)
Some Rain Must Fall and Other Stories by Michael Faber (Canongate
  2000)
The Difficulties of the Bridegroom by Ted Hughes (Faber and Faber,
  1996)
Complete Short Stories by Franz Kafka (Vintage, 2008)
The New Granta Book of the American Short Story, Ed: R Ford (Granta
  2007)
Ovid Metamorphosed, Ed: P Terry (Vintage 2001)
East, West by Salman Rushdie (Vintage 1998)
The Stories of Eva Luna by Isabelle Allende (Penguin 1992)

 IDEAS FOR FURTHER EXPLORATION

ONCE UPON A TIME

Write your life story as a fairy tale. What gifts (physical or
emotional) have you been blessed with—who gave them to you?
What did the bad fairy at the Christening feast curse you with—
psoriasis? Shyness? Envy? Cast some of the other characters as

though they were immortal/supernatural/uncanny. Let go of feeling silly or self-conscious—be outrageous—have fun.

MYTHICAL TRANSPOSITION

Research a mythical figure and plonk them into modern life. Perhaps Echo could be interviewed by a psychiatrist in hospital— or Hera could appear on Daytime TV, telling her errant husband She's Had Enough . . . maybe Bacchus has bought up every wine retailer in the country . . .

IMAGINE THE IMPOSSIBLE

Give a fictional character a strange gift/curse—everything they touch becomes invisible; they return from the dead to tut over wedding arrangements. Or perhaps an entire village population wakes up one day to find all the bigots have bright blue noses . . .

ADAM MAREK

WHAT MY GLAND WANTS — ORIGINALITY IN THE SHORT STORY

W hen I read or write fiction, what I'm really doing is hunting for a very particular sensation. It's a feeling a bit like delight, a bit like surprise, a bit like weightlessness. It's the excitement we get when we discover something new, something which in childhood we can't take a step without tripping over, but which in adulthood is woefully infrequent.

I get this sensation most intensely when I'm reading or writing short fiction.

Something about this form lends itself to revelation. I can think of many moments when I have just finished reading a short story, and am sitting on my knackered sofa holding the book in my hands, too caught up in it, too exhausted by the ideas it has put into my head, to even think about reading another one.

This sensation is particular to short stories, for me anyway. The pleasures a novel has to give are meted out in the course of its journey, and all too often, when I finish the last line of a novel

I've been living with for weeks, I'm left with a feeling of emptiness. Oh. So that's how it ends? Novels tail off at their close, slowing letting us out. The abrupt nature of short stories, good ones anyway, sees our heads thrust into a bucket of cold water and then just as quickly pulled out again leaving us gasping for air. We have to take a moment afterwards for everything to settle again. It is this moment of settling that is the signature mark of a great story.

Of course there are so many pleasures to be had from a novel that a short can never give us, but this is a book about the short form, so I want to say a bit about what the short story can do that the novel cannot. The short, that inquisitive little reptile, can scurry into holes that its chubby friend can only sigh at.

THE STORY GLAND

I think people who enjoy short stories have a special gland, one that responds to the unexpected with little bursts of pleasure chemicals. I have heard many writers describe short stories as 'addictive'. I think it's the stuff that this gland releases which we are addicted to.

I'm always suspicious of people who love to read, but who don't like short stories. These people, I think, if they have the gland, have a shrivelled thing, an atrophied little apple core. I pity these people. They are missing out on these inky little orgasms.

ABSURDITY

There are plenty of shorts which are poignant and beautiful vignettes that recognise the complexities of life in the smallest moments. But for me, the stories that make the most of the form, that get my gland salivating, are the ones that present me with something I've never seen before, something absurd, and then draw around it an internal logic—which justifies its existence, which makes it not just crazy surrealism, but grounds it in reality. In the spectrum of short fiction, it's stuff at the weird end that I most like to read and most like to write.

There's a level of absurdity you can get away with in a short that you can't get close to with a novel. The short story reader has the ability to suspend their disbelief to a far greater degree— they accept that all superfluities have been stripped from the story, that explanations may be withheld to serve the greater good—the delivery of a single idea. Something miraculous in a matchbox.

Once you start extending the length of a short story, adding to that single idea you want to convey, you have to start adding scaffolding to hold it in place. Novels need a lot of scaffolding. Every action within a story requires a motivation and a consequence. As soon as you begin to add more characters and more actions, the number of consequences rapidly multiplies, and the length grows exponentially. Short stories work because they're really about one action and its consequence.

ORIGINALITY

Originality is the most important thing in fiction for me. My gland needs things it has never experienced before. And when I'm thinking about ideas for a short story, it's my gland that I'm guided by. I get ideas for stories every day, but when presented with the majority of them, my gland shrugs and goes back to sleep. When I come up with an idea that works, I get a physical sensation. A strange kind of adrenaline. Sometimes I giggle. Sometimes I need to go to the toilet. This is my sign that I'm on to something.

I don't believe in *absolute* originality. There is no such thing as a purely original idea BUT . . . there is an infinite number of original confluences of ideas. Originality lies in the meeting of two things which have never met before. Or more than two things. When things that have never met before are melded successfully in the short story, they give off little static charges. It's these charges that our gland is so fond of, and often, they're found in the first line of the story.

Take this one, from Alison MacLeod's story 'Discharge':

> When my wife, Angelina, is aroused, ball lightning slides from between her legs: a sphere of plasma, sometimes the size of an orange, sometimes the size of a basketball.

BANG. Pleasure chemicals.

Or this first line from Kafka's *The Metamorphosis*:

As Gregor Samsa awoke one morning from uneasy dreams he found himself transformed in his bed into a gigantic insect.

Awesome.

I get the most pleasure from reading short stories where known things are combined to form something unknown. People wake up and are bugs. Ball lightning comes out of girls' fannies.

WHAT DOES IT ALL MEAN?

When I write short stories, it's this alien cocktail of ideas that I'm pursuing, but like the examples above, there has to be a reason to collide these ideas. The chimera you have created has to stand for something — it has to represent more than just the sum of its parts. Weirdness for the sake of weirdness is just masturbation. When the oddity in a story is a way to talk about or expose some human truth which we have all experienced, that's when our gland really begins to sing.

And sometimes the gland knows what the meaning of the story is, even if we don't 'get it' consciously. Sometimes the truth a story is revealing is too diaphanous for us to say 'ah yes, this story was about x' and enable us to relate its meaning to some-one else. Sometimes, we have a sense of understanding it uncon-sciously — and this I believe is the moment when we finish a story and cannot move until everything settles again, while our unconscious mind finishes chewing and swallows it.

I often experience the same thing when I'm writing. A particu-lar confluence of ideas will feel right, but I won't be able to see what it's really *about* until I've finished the first draft and read it back. And then when I rewrite, I'll hone it to make that meaning resonate.

Writers often say that when it goes well, it does it all by itself, actually, maybe it was Bruce Lee who said that, but anyhoo, there are moments when the experience of writing is almost like sitting in the passenger seat watching someone else do it. And if this is the unconscious part of us steering the wheel, it sometimes has a destination that we don't get to know about until we get there.

AN EXAMPLE

I was driving to my in-laws in North London with my iPod on shuffle, and 'Hey Jude' by the Beatles came on. I got this vivid image of a zombie foot tapping to the music. My gland really dug that. While my wife took our boys into her parents' place, I stayed in the car listening to 'Hey Jude' a few more times, seeing for the first time that it was a great anthem for zombies.

I noticed that in this image, the foot was tapping on a tiled floor next to the leg of a cheap table, and my gland got really excited when it realised the zombie was in a restaurant.

The zombie foot tapping became the end scene of 'Meaty's Boys', the last story in my collection *Instruction Manual for Swallowing*. It's about a guy who works in a restaurant for zombies.

It was the combination of zombies and a restaurant that had my gland dancing. It was something I'd never seen before. It wasn't until after I'd written four or five scenes that I realised the story was really about peer pressure, about how someone can be persuaded out of their comfort zone, into dangerous and terrifying territory, by the members of the group they belong to. I then went back to the beginning and rewrote with this in mind.

THE PERFECT SHORT STORY

For me, the test of a really effective short story is to ask whether it could be extrapolated to a novel. If a story could only have been told as a short, then it has made the most effective use of the medium and is most likely to get our gland excited.

Of course there are lots of brilliant short stories that do not follow this rule, whose characters could very easily take another step after the final word, and another, and so on. But there's something very special about the short story that would destroy itself if it stretched to another sentence. It has been said that in a perfect short story, there should not be a single word that could be taken away. I take this also to mean that the perfect story would be ruined if a single word were added. That it has reached its ultimate size and complexity.

Short stories are like bubbles. Their existence is brief and miraculous, but the stuff that makes them can only attain a certain size. Once you want your bubbles to get bigger, or to last longer, you have to start using different materials. You have to start stitching pieces together. Seamlessness is only possible within the short story. Perfection is only possible within the short story. And it is the pursuit of perfection, the balanced equation where everything that is included supports everything else and nothing could possibly be removed or added, that keeps us reading them.

 ## FAVOURITE SHORT STORIES

'Billennium' by J.G. Ballard from *The Complete Short Stories* (Flamingo, 2002)

'The Metamorphosis' by Franz Kafka from *The Complete Short Stories* (Vintage Classics, 1999)

'Z.Z.'s Sleep-Away Camp for Disordered Dreamers' by Karen Russell from *St. Lucy's Home for Girls Raised by Wolves* (Chatto and Windus, 2007)

'Discharge' by Alison MacLeod from *Fifteen Modern Tales of Attraction* (Penguin, 2007)

'The Rise and Fall of Sharpie Cakes' by Haruki Murakami from *Blind Willow, Sleeping Woman* (Harvill Secker, 2006)

'The Angel' by Patrick McGrath from *Blood and Water and Other Stories* (Penguin, 1992)

'The Numbers' by Clare Wigfall from *The Loudest Sound and Nothing* (Faber and Faber, 2007)

'So Proud' by Robert Shearman from *Tiny Deaths* (Comma Press, 2007)

'Lions in Winter' by Wena Poon from *Lions in Winter* (Salt, 2009)

'Hat Trick' by Etgar Keret from *Missing Kissinger* (Chatto and Windus, 2007)

i IDEAS FOR FURTHER EXPLORATION

Keep lists of words that intrigue you for some reason. Two lists: those words you respond favourably to, and those you don't. It could be because of their sounds, their connotations, anything. Pick at random a word from each list, and marry them into the title of a story. And write the story . . .

TOBIAS HILL

CHARACTER, CHARACTERISATION, DIALOGUE AND LANGUAGE

AN INTERVIEW

VANESSSA GEBBIE: Talk to me about character in your work? Some people say 'story is character'. Is that so for you?

TOBIAS HILL: I think there are two distinct ways of writing, each of them suited to different writers in greater or lesser proportions. But we have to be able to use both methods. Firstly, you can begin in a structured way, knowing where you are going, more or less, knowing roughly what is going to happen and in what sequence, before you start. I would call that plot-based writing. On the other hand, you can improvise and let a character run ahead of you, simply writing what happens to that character as it happens, and I would call that character-led writing, where the character is calling the shots for the duration.

I find that second way very energising. It lifts the process, adds a bit of excitement. It's a lovely feeling when a character starts doing unplanned things. You know they are 'alive' then.

GEBBIE: I agree, it is. So which type of writer are you, would you say? Do you tend to work in a plot-driven way, or an intuitive character-led way?

HILL: I do some of both. And I find that each method creates its own friction, and a third friction builds up between the two processes, if used side by side. That's the point, really. I think it is also a matter of temperament, which type of writing suits us best. I am suited to both, but tend to plan more than I allow my characters to run. I suppose if you look at structured writing as a continuum, where 'no structure' is 1 and 'total adherence to plot' is 10, I must be about at 7 on this Richter Scale.

I would say that it is important not to try to know everything, though. That makes the writing process rather mechanical.

But here I ought to say I am drawing a comparison between novels and short stories. You see, when you are writing a novel you have so much time, and space. You can afford to let your characters take off and you can afford not to plan too rigidly. In the short story, for a writer like me, at any rate, I have to have some planning done before I start. To have a map, if you like. One of the things I enjoy with short stories is the possibility of seeing the light at the end of the tunnel early on. Seeing the ending, perhaps, before you even start writing.

GEBBIE: I understand that. I often have a final tableau in my head, and I let my characters take me towards that ending. Often though, they surprise me. The tableau is as I saw it, but it means something different in the context of the story.

HILL: I think the ending is far more important in a short story than in a novel. So often you ask someone what the final scene was in a novel, and they can't tell you. Whereas a good short story—the ending stays with you for a long time.

GEBBIE: They can be just perfect, can't they? Can you give me an example of a perfect ending?

HILL: Absolutely. Here again, something that the short story is so good for. In short stories as with poetry, the writer can try to aim at perfection. To produce something absolutely perfect. That's a huge advantage of short stories. The writer simply can't aim at perfection in writing a novel. It is too big. There will be something not quite right if it is analysed, I think.

The example I'd give here is 'A Small Good Thing' by Raymond Carver. The ending of that story is deceptively simple, and absolutely perfect.

GEBBIE: Can you say something about how it feels when a character 'takes off' and starts running ahead of the writer? How does a writer know when that is happening?

HILL: The whole process becomes a lot more energised. A 'switch' happens, when the character picks up the baton, and some of the rise in energy comes from my knowledge that something is working well . . . that character has sprung into life. Is not merely 'my creation' as I planned him/her to be. So I am not having to second-guess what the character will do or say. It is a hugely energising process for me when that happens, the character lives and is full of surprises.

GEBBIE: The short story, as you say, has little time and space to flesh out characters for the reader, and yet so often the intensity of the short story experience leaves a character and his journey in the reader's head long after the story is put down.

Can you say a little about the craft behind this skill? Can you talk about how you bring your characters to life?

HILL: It has to do with the characters in short stories being 'minor' characters. But that needs explaining.

How many novels do you read where the central character is actually the weakest in terms of craft, and really hard to pin down if someone asked you to describe them as a person? I find many 'major' characters actually rather hollow when I try to think about them. So often it is the more peripheral characters that are stronger in terms of image, personality, motivation — those things that we can catch hold of and remember as readers.

I think it is because the author is so often so close to the central character, in many ways, it is an embodiment of him / herself, and therefore he assumes an understanding about that character that the reader cannot have. He doesn't fill in the gaps, and leaves the character hollow even though he might take up a lot of 'writing space'. If you like, I am saying that in a short story there is no room for a single hollow central character that is the equivalent of the major protagonist in a novel.

Moving away from this central character, to the minor 'more artificial' ones (if we look at them as extensions of the writer) . . . the novel author allows himself to take shortcuts, to use carica-ture, even use a touch of stereotype. You will find many of the minor characters are drawn far better, sharp and clear. These are the ones that will correspond to the central characters in the short story.

So, the central characters in the short story may be drawn in a similar way. It is a technique that relies on the prior knowledge of the reader. To use elements of caricature or stereotype—both clichés—assumes the reader understands the code, and therefore understands the main characteristics of the character without the writer necessarily having to explain them.

GEBBIE: That's interesting—I am mentally comparing this with so many exhortations I have read and heard, saying a writer must endeavour never to use stereotypes and clichés! Tell me more.

HILL: The thing about careful use of cliché in characterisation is that the writer is in control of how far to go. Think about it. What is a cliché, a stereotype? A comparison that has become old, and lost its edge. Reasons *not* to use them in your writing are good and obvious. They are not fresh, they are tired, hackneyed images, and to litter your work with them is disastrous. But to help a short story writer paint character fast, their use with a light hand is a useful tool

They are used precisely because they hold a resonant potency, and I think it is worth remembering that, not dismissing them completely. Especially when creating character in short fiction. There is an immediate recognition in the mind of the reader, tried and tested characteristics for the reader to latch onto fast, giving them a sense of the character quickly.

It's a technique Charles Dickens used a lot. But he went too far with this one for the modern palate.

I do think there is a danger these days in not using any recognisable brushstrokes. We are in danger of creating wishy-washy characters because we just don't have the space in the short story to do otherwise. We avoid the clichés, and end up with vagueness, which is just as bad!

GEBBIE: Can you give me an example of this technique in your own short stories?

HILL: Yes. In my collection *Skin* (Faber and Faber, 1997) there is a story called 'Brolly'. It is very short, five or six pages. A group of adults is on top of a hill drinking, recalling a somewhat depraved family game they used to play. They are watching their youngsters playing this same game at the foot of the hill. One of the adults is now the grandmother. And she is simply based on the archetypal old English lady, and I am trusting that my reader will have a handle on what that is.

In this story I have eight characters in five pages to play with. There is almost no time at all to 'introduce' them. The grandmother, whilst she is obviously important or she would not be there, does not need to be anything other than this within the context of this story. Indeed, I would argue, had I made her anything else, the reader would have followed that thread for a while, rather than stick to the story line I wanted. It would have muddied and confused, rather than clarified.

So yes, I rely on a 'stock' older English lady, and lift her into life via gesture and dialogue. It only then takes a few tiny things —one physical characteristic, for example—to create 'my' character, as opposed to all the others she might be.

GEBBIE: You mention your use of dialogue. Can you say something about this?

HILL: I think it is important to understand that there is a fundamental difference in intent between dialogue in real life and dialogue in fiction.

In real life, we use dialogue to communicate information. But, if you try to write fictional dialogue like that, you end up with what I call the Star Trek script:

Scotty: Shall we progress at Warp factor three, Captain?

Captain Kirk: Oh no, Scotty. Don't you remember, last week, when we progressed in this area of space at Warp factor three, we flew into that megatronic dust cloud?

Etc etc

It's sheer information dump. Some writing teachers talk about dialogue being good because it is showing not telling. Not in this case!

In fiction however, dialogue is one of the main characterisation tools at the writer's disposal. I would say it is its main function. So I see dialogue as an adjunct of characterisation, not plot. It does of course have a lesser function, that of dramatisation, moving the plot forward.

Invariably, if a writer uses dialogue purely as a conveyor of information, it sounds clunky, and inorganic.

GEBBIE: Whose work would you use as an example of great dialogue?

HILL: Raymond Carver, again. He had real skill here. If you analyse a section of dialogue from one of his short stories, you will see how he uses their speech to create characters who are just not good at talking to each other. They are mis-communicators.

GEBBIE: What about physical characteristics? How important is it for a reader to be told what a character looks like?

HILL: Well, if we go back to the 'hollow' central characters in novels that I was talking about earlier, how often do you find that they are not actually described? And is that because they are so close to being the author that the author does not want to describe himself?

For me, if a character has no description at all, it only adds to the hollowness. I think you do need to have something. A single physical characteristic perhaps, something to define this character. Something seemingly small, but salient.

I think of it like this: having physical description in your characterisation toolkit is like having the salt beside you when you are cooking. You don't need a lot of it, indeed, use too much and you ruin the dish. But it is necessary to have just enough. One key detail, as I said. Something to distinguish this character from the others.

And it works both ways. For the reader, it fleshes out the character. Gives the character something fresh and different to 'wear', for the reader to 'see' and associate with that character. And for the writer, it frees the character up a little, distances that character from the writer and makes it easier for him to take on a life of his own.

GEBBIE: Do you have an example from your work? A story in which you use this craft particularly well, looking back?

HILL: There is one short story, a longer one of about fifty five pages, set in a zoo in which bodies of dead animals go missing. The story opens with a girl in the shower. She can't get rid of the scent of the animals from her reddened skin. The heat shows up scar tissue, she thinks about the animals shut in at night, and is reminded of prison. Her hair falls forward in a long dark rope. And that's about it. But in that little scene, you meet a character, have hints about her back story, a little about her physical appearance but not much. The hair is important; it will come into focus later in the work.

GEBBIE: **Fantastic example. So many senses must come into play here. Description gives the writer a chance to show language skills too, don't they? But isn't it so easy to get those wrong, just as it is easy to use the wrong language in dialogue? A story from a child's point of view, for example. Isn't there an argument that says the writer should only consider using vocabulary that the child would reasonably know?**

HILL: But we have a tradition of story-telling and the storyteller uses the language of the storyteller! Aren't you over-complicating things?

I think about the work of Angela Carter here. She used incredibly rich, extravagant, theatrical language. The current movement tends to be cleaner-cut. Contemporary writing tends to be more Carveresque. I appreciate both of them. But on the whole, I would say I go for simplicity, and enjoy the move away from heavier literary 'latinate' language.

Think about it. Don't policemen sound faintly ridiculous when they talk on *Crimewatch*?

At three in the afternoon on the subsequent day, I apprehended the perpetrator after a brief altercation.

It's arcane and indecipherable, sometimes. I prefer to read work written in everyday language, especially (underlined!) in dialogue. Yes, here, the characters have to use the words the characters would use. It sounds such a truism. Almost silly to say it, isn't it?

Latinate language is lovely in the right dosage. Back to Angela Carter here. Her early work is now almost unreadable because she crams in so much. But 'The Bloody Chamber' onwards, about 1979, onwards — she feels comfortable in her own skin. The language can still be rich, but she chooses where to put the gems. When she does use a beautiful word, it stands out so well, like a well-set jewel.

So generally, I would advocate writing simply when you are learning. Don't try to be writerly because it just gets in the way of the story.

GEBBIE: You have given writers so much to think about here, and some seriously useful advice. Thank you so very much!

 ## FAVOURITE SHORT STORIES

The stories of Raymond Carver, for their superb characterisation and dialogue.

IDEAS FOR FURTHER EXPLORATION

ONE

Go somewhere you can sit quietly and listen to how people speak to each other. Make notes. Notice the 'ums' and the 'ahs', the unfinished sentences. Take notes, or if possible, record snatches of conversation, and then transcribe them exactly. Would they work as dialogue in a good short story? If not, why not?

TWO

Take a few paragraphs of exposition from a published short story, or indeed from one of your own short stories. And then rewrite those paragraphs as direct speech from a main character. Allow them to put the information contained in the paragraphs in their own words. Redo, using a different character.

Create a scene where the two characters discuss the information given, 'offstage' as it were. Does anything different emerge?

SARAH SALWAY

STEALING STORIES

And yet the only exciting life is the imaginary one

VIRGINIA WOOLF

The university in which I teach creative writing has a popular reading series. On the day I start writing this chapter, I turn up early to find the guest poet waiting nervously in the lecture room. He's chewing his nails and wondering what questions he might get. 'They'll definitely want to know where you get your ideas from,' I say.

Brian groans because it's the one question all writers get asked the most, but as it happens, the reading doesn't even reach the question and answer stage. Early on, when he is reading a poem about walking on a beach, a member of the audience stands up and starts declaiming a poem of his own about the sea but at a much louder volume. Brian starts to chew his nails again as the heckler is escorted out, but he manages to start another poem, this time about his daughter's birth, when yet another audience member stands up to read a rival poem about childbirth.

The third time this happens, the reading is called to a halt. Brian hardly has any nails left by this time and is swearing never to write again, so I never do get to find out where he did get his ideas from.

But it's an interesting question, because where *do* we get our ideas from? Or more specifically, *how* do we get our ideas? One myth is that ideas come to artists magically, floating in from our unconscious, our dreams, or that we are somehow born with a treasure chest of ideas to sift through. When I first started to write, I had an urgency to my writing that makes me wonder now if I was scared my particular treasure chest might run out.

A more honest answer though is that we gather many of our story ideas from other people. From our friends, family, the people we work alongside, newspapers, snatches of conversation we overhear, myths and legends, text books, the list goes on. But it still takes a brave writer to admit this in public, one such as T S Eliot who proudly declared, 'Mediocre writers borrow; great writers steal'.

It's the difference between borrowing and stealing that is the crux here. To borrow a car is to expect to give it back intact, but if you steal it, then you need to find some way of making it your own. Professionals can quickly make any car unrecognisable by painting it pink, maybe, or turning it into spare parts. And so with stories. A good writing process is such that when we take a story from someone else, we will use our imagination and work and work on the original story until, in the final draft, the original owners probably won't be able to recognise it either.

We have made it our own.

Painted it pink. Stripped it for spare parts.

And in doing so, we've made sense of it for ourselves.

It's the latter that makes the stealing so compulsive. The motivation behind my thefts has never been to deprive someone else of what they own, but to understand what it is about their stories that has captured my imagination so strongly.

For the purpose of this chapter, I've taken three categories of stories that can be stolen: stranger's stories you overhear or are told, family stories that often happened long before we were born, and newspaper stories. The two central links are firstly, that we were not involved in any way within the story, and secondly there is something about them that won't leave us alone, even if it can take weeks, months or even years before we find the right fictional vehicle to explore them.

STORIES ABOUT STRANGERS

One of my stories, 'Painting the Family Pet', came from a telephone conversation with a friend about an artist she knew who knocked on people's doors, offering to paint their pets. She had got so tired of people saying they had no pets that, one day, she offered to paint their furniture instead.

After I'd put down the phone, I couldn't stop thinking about why someone would want to have their furniture painted. Later, when I went into the kitchen to make some tea, a story came to me about a woman who was so obsessed with food that she commissions a portrait of her fridge. Although the final story is told from the point of view of the fridge's owner, the original anecdote allowed me to think of the artist's motivations too. Both women wanted something from one another. Because I didn't know the people involved, I wrote around the image I was left with after the phone call—an artist setting up her easel in front of a piece of household furniture, having to take it just as seriously as any human portrait.

In a *Paris Review* interview,[1] Raymond Carver gives the original inspiration behind his story, 'Why Don't You Dance?'.

> We were all sitting around drinking and someone told a story about a barmaid named Linda who got drunk with her boyfriend one night and decided to move all of her bedroom furnishings into the backyard. They did it, too, right down to the carpet and the bedroom lamp, the bed, the nightstand, everything. There were about four or five writers in the room, and after the guy finished telling the story, someone said, 'Well, who's going to write it?'

It took Carver more than four years to write his own version, in which a newly separated man puts his possessions on his front lawn to see if they look any better outside than inside. A young couple come and end up dancing amongst the objects—a facsimile of the happiness the owner must have once hoped his things would bring. What makes 'Why Don't You Dance?' all Carver's is that, although the seed of the idea came from the drunken anecdote, he infuses his story with what he describes as his main theme:

> It's their (his characters) lives they've become uncomfortable with, lives they see breaking down. They'd like to set things right, but they can't. And usually they do know it, I think, and after that they just do the best they can.[2]

'Why Don't You Dance?', the first story Carver wrote after he gave up drinking, is full of fictional details that separate it from the original — almost humorous — image of the drunken barmaid. Carver raises the story's stakes by changing the protagonist to a man in a state of crisis, while the device of the observing couple highlights how other people can't help him either. His pain won't go away just because he's exposed it in his yard along with his furniture. The girl in the story can't shake off her reaction to what happened that night.

> Weeks later, she said: 'The guy was about middle-aged. All his things right there in his yard. No lie. We got real pissed and danced. In the driveway. Oh, my God. Don't laugh. He played us these records. Look at this record-player. The old guy give it to us, and all these crappy records. Will you look at this shit?'
>
> She kept talking. She told everyone. There was more to it, and she was trying to get it talked out. After a time, she quit trying. [2]

Given that it took Carver several years from first hearing the story to writing it, it's possible to believe that something in the picture of an anonymous barmaid's possessions out on the lawn caused the same reaction in him as his character. He needed to get it written out into some sort of meaning for himself.

FAMILY STORIES

Old family story are a great source for material, not least because we are often only told half the story and our imagination is already working to supply the rest. Edinburgh writer Jo Swingler has never forgotten being told by her mother about four Australian monks who turned up out of the blue in an ambulance to visit her grandmother in the 60s. Swingler's mother had no idea who the monks were, so working with just this fragment, Swingler wrote her story, 'Not Even An Ambulance Can Save You'.[3] Four monks in an ambulance is the kind of arresting picture that would be hard to conjure up from nothing, and the good news is that nearly every family contains similar stories. Over the years, when I've asked people, I've been told fantastic stories including a man who built two identical houses on top of the same hill but facing out different directions because his wife couldn't decide which view she liked best, an overly superstitious great aunt who ended up wrecking the marriage she was trying to save because she was too busy making spells, and a gossip who would get into strangers' cars at traffic lights in order to have a conversation with them.

The stories of prize-winning writer, Jhumpa Lahiri, all have a strong theme running through them. Her characters struggle so vividly with loss and the yearnings of exile in both her collections, *Interpreter of Maladies* and *Unaccustomed Earth* and are full of so many complicated and believable emotions, that it's not surprising to find out that at least one of her stories, 'The Third and Final Continent', came directly from a story her father used to tell about the time he had rented a house from a one-hundred-

and-three-year-old woman who loved to talk about all the men who had been to the moon.

Although these details — and more — found their way into Lahiri's story, she makes the story emphatically hers.

> I think the difference is that I am at such a remove . . . I have no idea what it's like to immigrate, I have no idea what it's like to be a man. I have no idea what it was like for my father . . . even though all of these details were given to me in terms of family history, I had to work extra hard to make them ring true, and to make them credible. [4]

The work paid off because when Lahiri showed her father the story, he simply said, 'My whole life is there.'

Although we often hear that every writer has a 'splinter of ice in their heart', when I use my own family's stories in my fiction, I am often terrified about the reactions they will have to the end result. I want to use these stories not just because some of them are just too good to go unrecorded but more importantly, as the first form of story-telling I came across, they are part of my narrative history. However, by publishing them under my name, I can't help feeling that I am claiming ownership of them in a way that's different from all us sitting round at parties and celebrations, taking it in turns to tell the same stories time and time again.

I haven't worked out an easy answer to this, apart from the fact that my need to explore this material is so strong that I know I will be telling the stories my own way. Not the way my brothers might, or my sister. Writing to understand my life, and that of others, has always been a primary aim — and privilege — of my writing practice. And it has certainly got easier, although there are still arguments over many of the details I use. One of my characters in my first novel, *Something Beginning With*, has to wear a coat made from leftover hunting pink material, and this led to many discussions between my siblings over whether the garment our ancestor was supposedly forced to wear was actually a coat or a jacket. In the end, I had to say, 'it's my story'.

I know that every time I worry too much over what other people will think, my writing becomes stilted and self-justifying. The only way I can get round this is to write the first draft as if no one will read it. It's only in the editing process, when I have worked out what I need to say, that I make decisions as to what to put in and what to leave out. I want to show respect for the other people involved so sometimes, however reluctantly, I have to admit that particular stories aren't mine to tell. Or perhaps it's not the right time to tell.

Even then, like the coat or jacket question, you can't always spot what will annoy people most. One of my first short stories was based on my father's memories of the first new car he owned. However, I had my character leave the car out in the drive to show it off, something my father swore he never did. Similarly, Swingler didn't expect her mother to get upset about how the grandmother in the ambulance story served Spam sandwiches to the monks.

'I'd used this as a way of placing the story in a specific time,' said Swingler, 'but she said my nan would never have used Spam; ever! This detail really jarred with her.' [5]

However, Swingler kept the Spam sandwiches in her story, just as I left the car out of the garage, and Lahiri changed chronological details in her father's story so that the day her character landed in Britain was the same day that Neil Armstrong first walked on the moon. When we take something from life, our attempts to be faithful to the facts often get in the way of the story we need to write. We lose sight of the bigger picture, and by crying, 'but it really happened', we forget that emotional truths can be more important than facts. By connecting the moon landing to her father's first experiences in Britain, Lahiri shows just what a huge step it is to move to a new country:

> ... it was so much a part of my family lore that it's one of those things you feel so close to, you can't see it. It was only after I had spent quite a bit of time wrestling with the making of the story that it occurred to me that it was such a fascinating confluence of events—one very personal and one so very, very public that changed the world and how human beings think of themselves in relation to the rest of the universe. It was very gratifying to discover.[6]

NEWSPAPER STORIES

Flicking through my local newspaper, my attention is drawn to an article about a woman who was taken for a spin round Brands Hatch for her 106th birthday. Although she was driven at speeds of more than 100 miles an hour, she still complained that it wasn't fast enough. It's a great story, and one I cut out to keep in my files.

When a story is taken from a news article, the facts are not normally in dispute. What becomes interesting then is the 'affected facts'—how they will affect other people. This is when the fiction writer's mantra, 'what if?' comes into play to write the next stage of the story.

What if it were my father who had been caught coming out of a sex shop on CCTV? What if the baby taken hostage was never told about it but, after he's grown up, he meets his kidnapper by accident one day? What if the army veterans offered a free coach trip ended up organising one last ambush along the way?

What if the 106-year-old woman leaves a will laying out exactly what risks she wants her safety conscious family to take?

Another powerful version of a story can come from giving a voice to a silent participant. Joyce Carol Oates did this with the teenager, Connie, in her story, 'Where are You Going, Where Have You Been?', which was based on a newspaper report Oates had read about a young girl's murder. [7]

When Kim Edwards read a story in the *Des Moines Register* about a protest against a mid-western abortion clinic, it was the image of children used symbolically by the protestors that wouldn't leave her alone.

> For days I kept thinking of those children, their small limbs and shiny hair, their tender skin pressed against the hot asphalt, the dip and weight of a car turning into the driveway. How had any group of adults come to find this scene acceptable? [8]

At first, she resisted turning it into fiction because she was concerned about entering a political minefield. But then out driving one day, after weeks of thinking about the protest, a first line suddenly popped into her head, 'You'd know me if you saw me.' She stopped the car outside a library, and rushed in to write the first opening pages of her story, 'The Story of My Life'. She'd found the story's voice. Or the answer to that magic question beloved of writing tutors: 'Who is telling the story?' Edwards goes on:

> In literature we tend to care about the political only to the extent that it touches and shapes the individual lives of characters. Stories aren't about issues, they're about people . . . I'd urge any writer to embrace what's happening in the world—absolutely, don't look away—but also to know quite clearly going into the narrative whose story is needing to be told, and why.

This different take on a story—an unexpected narrator, an unusual emphasis, a passion to tell a particular as opposed to an abstract truth—helps to keep a story fresh. And just as we ask the question, 'who' is telling the story, we also need to ask 'why'. What are our own writerly themes that make someone else's story worth telling our particular way? And perhaps more importantly, *why* won't this story leave us alone? What image is in it, what message does it have, that keeps it turning over and over in our mind? The good news is that are as many answers to these questions as there are writers. And none of them are wrong.

WHY STEAL?

The original idea behind this chapter came from a short fiction anthology I contributed to which was called, appropriately, *Stolen Stories*.[9] All the writers in the collection had thieved their stories in one way or another, and we had to confess to our 'nature of theft'. These reports make fascinating reading. My story was written as a birthday present. I was given five words that had significance to the recipient, but I had no idea what this was. The more I wrote, the more it felt as if I was taking away their meaning from her by making them my own. Another contributor, Lindsay Bower, was inspired by a glamorous childhood friend who skipped school to buy a lottery ticket. Bower recalls how she was in 'complete awe' of this girl because, in the unlikely event of her missing school as a teenager, it would have been to spend more time reading. Now many years later, she writes a first person account of lottery ticket buying and teenage drinking and relives the past in a different way. Nicole Reid also fulfils old wishes through her story, 'Red Wagon'. Reid's inspiration came from a conversation she had with Richard Bausch about how his wife once wore a red dress when she waited for him. Reid admits:

> The sun on the red of her dress was the colour of love, was something I wanted and had no idea how to make mine. So I wrote about it. [10]

It's this fierce desire for something in the story—an emotion, an understanding, a voice—that allows us to change characters, places, motivations, even what sandwiches were eaten, and yet still retain its integrity. It's also what makes our version new and fresh. Just as I'm still amazed at how exactly the same exercise in a writing class will result in such diverse pieces every time, I also know that the story I write after overhearing two people talk is unique to me, even if another writer happens to hear and write about exactly the same conversation. Or that a piece I write in my father's voice about the tea set he brought home from the war, say, will be different from the piece my sister writes. Just so long as I write into it using my own truths.

Now a confession. Remember my initial story of what happened during the university reading? Well, I stole it. The real Brian wasn't heckled. He didn't even chew his nails once. We all listened quietly until we were asked if we had any questions. The story of audience members standing up to read their own poems against the official reader was something I was recently told that a group of Spanish writers used to do. It shocked and frightened me when I heard it because it connects to all the nightmares I have ever had about reading in public. Including the one where I'm booed off the stage. Actually especially that one. It was a relief to steal the story, turn it into my own and give it to Brian. Who probably would have been able to cope, but luckily didn't have to find out. As it happens, he also wasn't asked where he got his ideas from (although he *was* asked, somewhat surprisingly, if he was afraid of dying).

I, however, came out with a notebook buzzing with possible story ideas I'd harvested from the research and the anecdotes he generously shared with us from the stage.

Do I feel guilty? Do I heck. Give me a couple of weeks, some pink paint, and a parts stripper, and I will have made my random and almost illegible notes—*body leaking, life in objects, fear of being buried alive*—completely my own.

 FAVOURITE SHORT STORIES

'Cathedral' by Raymond Carver from *Cathedral* (Vintage, 2003)
'The Darling' by Anton Chekhov from *Lady With Lapdog* (Penguin
    Books, 1964)

'A Real Doll' by A M Homes from *Safety of Objects* (Harpers Perennial, 2003)

'Bullet in the Brain' by Tobias Wolff from *The Night in Question* (Vintage, 1997)

'In the Gloaming' by Alice Elliot Dark from *In the Gloaming* (Simon & Schuster, 2000)

 ## IDEAS FOR FURTHER EXPLORATION

FIND THE THEME

Take a story you have overheard or been told, and take it back to the bare events, eg *Artist—can't sell paintings—goes door to door—pet portraits—no-one has pets—paints furniture instead.* Now, think what it is about this story that interests you. Not what is generally interesting, but what interests YOU. This will be your theme. In my case, it was what happens when inanimate things replace a living, breathing love. Another writer might go off on a riff about wild animals in suburbia, or just how much luck is involved in being discovered as an artist. You might want to brainstorm several themes for the same story. Then pick one and rewrite the story your way following your theme. Take it further than your original list of events. What happened next? Who else is in the story? Start with an image that sums up your theme, such as the man watching the young couple dancing amongst his objects in Carver's story. In my story, 'Painting the Family Pet', the story begins with two desperate women on either side of a front door, each wanting to be where the other was.

MIXING PERSONAL AND PUBLIC

If you can't think of a family story, interview family members about their childhood until something jumps out at you. Then locate the story in time. Research what was going on in the wider world at the time the story took place—what were the big news stories, what music was being played, what were women wearing, men, what books were people reading, what were people eating, what were they talking about? Like Lahiri, make connections between the family story and the bigger world picture. Change the dates or the location if necessary, but looking at your family's personal story through the larger public story will help you see it in a different way. Start with . . . 'It was the year that . . . (public) and it was also the year that . . . . (private), ie *It was the year that a bomb went off in Harrods and it was also the year that my mother first met Mr Richards.* Keep swopping over between public and private and see where it takes you. This is your first draft. Keep telling yourself that no one will see it.

WHO IS TELLING THIS STORY?

Arm yourself with some sharp scissors and start cutting out news stories that spark your interest until you have a pile. Local newspapers are great for this because they tend to concentrate on stories about individual people. You can go through back copies in your local library (although of course you can't take your scissors there!). Then pick just one story. Make notes of all the different characters who aren't mentioned in the story. Does the 'have-a-go' hero have a wife, or boyfriend? A son who will go to school and boast about his father with unfortunate results? What about the victim? Or the attacker? Or the police officer who joined up to save people and has never had the opportunity? Can he bear his jealousy at the attention the hero is receiving? Keep thinking about these silent participants until you hear their voice, the first line, and then tell what happened from their point of view. 'Stories aren't about issues, they're about people.' Dive in.

END NOTES

1   Raymond Carver was interviewed by Mona Simpson and Lewis Buzbee in Winter 1983 for *The Paris Review* Interviews. In the Penguin edition, (1988), John Updike picks out this quote from Carver in his introduction: 'Good fiction is partly a bringing of the news from one world to another. That end is good in and of itself, I think.'

2   'Why Don't You Dance?' by Raymond Carver from *What We Talk About When We Talk About Love* (Vintage, 2003).

3   In *Stolen Stories* (Forest Publications, 2008), Jo Swingler says of her story, 'Not Even An Ambulance Can Save You', 'I have no idea who the monks were, neither does my mum.'

4   Interview with Jhumpa Lahiri by Paul Mandelbaum, *Twelve Short Stories and Their Making* (Persea Books, 2005).

5   Taken from a private email exchange with Jo Swingler for the purpose of this chapter.

6   See 4.

7   Ailsa Cox, *Writing Short Stories* (Routledge 2005)

8   *Twelve Short Stories and their Making*, see 4. In his introduction, Paul Mandelbaum describes how in their email interview, Edwards had described the 'dedicated, sometimes

perilous process of revision in which she had struggled to find the story's true path'.

9 *Stolen Stories* was the idea of Nick Holdstock, and published by the Edinburgh arts organisation, Forest Publications. He says that although they received many compelling anecdotes in the submission process, what they were looking for was something that 'did not merely tell you what happened, but gave you ways to think about it you did not expect'.

10 'Red Wagon', by Nicole Reid from *Stolen Stories* (Forest Publications, 2008). The story ends with these lines:

> She shuts her eyes but takes his long fingers to her mouth, kisses his ring, and opens her eyes. 'A sort of wish,' she says.
> 'For what?'
> 'For this, just this.'

ELIZABETH BAINES

TRUE STORY — REAL STORY — GOOD FICTION?

H ow exactly do you turn a real-life incident, with all its inconsistencies and loose ends, its lack of shape, into a well-
formed and aesthetically satisfying story?

This is a question which confronted me—and made me swal-
low quite hard—when I was on a 'virtual tour' with my collection of stories, *Balancing on the Edge of the World*, in which literary
bloggers interviewed me about the collection and my writing
generally. My questioner—I nearly wrote *inquisitor*—was the
editor of this book, Vanessa Gebbie, who astutely judged it a
burning question for many writers. She asked me to illustrate
with one particular story from the collection, 'Condensed
Metaphysics', which she knew from reading my blog was indeed
based on a real-life incident.

I swallowed hard because as a writer talking to readers I am
usually very wary of revealing the real-life triggers for my fiction
—I usually refuse to do so, in fact. For one thing, once certain
elements in a piece of fiction are identified as facts, then a reader
is tempted to take the whole work as factual. To admit to any

'real-life' component or basis of a story is to encourage mistaken biographical readings of the story as a whole. But it seems to me that claiming factual truthfulness for any element of fiction is in any case both beside the point and pretty impossible. Once real life has been through the mangle of a writer's perceptions and the transformative process of fiction, it's become something else altogether and can't easily be claimed as factual truth. Real life and imagination become so fused that fiction is much more than the sum of its parts, and it's not only reductive to try and break it into its 'components', a denial of its transcendence, but quite hard anyway I find, after a piece is written, to remember precisely which is which.

Nevertheless, as Vanessa had noted, I had already made this mistake with 'Condensed Metaphysics'. Against my better judgment, and tickled by the acuity of the magazine editor who had agreed to publish it and had guessed that it did indeed have a real-life stimulus, I'd admitted that this was the case. Due to some crossed wires, but also I believe to the fact that by admitting this I'd invited him to see the whole thing as fact, to my great dismay he had subsequently published it as reportage. I recounted this publishing experience on my blog, precisely to show how misleading and dangerous it can be to discuss the 'real-life' aspects of fiction, and to explain how the story was most certainly fiction rather than fact—which, ironically, did of course involve some teasing out of the 'real-life' bits and those I had made up.

But Vanessa wanted to know precisely *how* I had turned the incident into fiction. How had I made those choices—what to take from the real-life incident, what to leave out and what to make up? How had I come to that alchemical fusion of real life and imagination which makes a piece of fiction? It's a question which moves us onto a deeper level of discussion altogether, and in answering it for Vanessa's blog I came to see that it concerns matters not only of craft but also of how we as writers creating fictions relate to reality in general. Trying to work out exactly how I used the incident to make 'Condensed Metaphysics' made me realize that to some extent, even while I was inside the situation, I was already subconsciously making a story out of it: to a certain extent what I was looking at already was not so much objective reality as the story I was starting to create.

So how did it happen, and how did the process of story-making develop after I consciously saw the incident as a possible story and then wrote it?

'Condensed Metaphysics' is the story of a group of people out on the town in the late evening and ending up in a place that is identifiable if you know it: a pizza takeaway on the university stretch of Manchester's Oxford Road. This is how it begins:

> We're all drunk and Ellie's drunkest. She runs up to a guy with a begging cup outside the Babylon and asks him to lend us some money, we're hungry and want a pizza and none of us has got any cash.
>
> He's about her own age, nineteen. He shakes his head matter-of-factly in his tight woolly hat. He doesn't find her request unreasonable. He holds out his styrofoam cup to show us only a few coins.

Ellie and the homeless guy get talking and he gives a long philosophical speech, comical yet moving I hope, about his own situation and humanity in general. Then the group of friends goes off into the Babylon to buy pizzas with a card—Ellie promising the homeless guy that they'll buy him one—to encounter a group of odd-ball characters with whom they have more comical yet ultimately serious discussion centering on the fact that everyone in the room mishears one of them, a researcher, as saying that he's researching 'condensed metaphysics'. When the group are finally tucking into their pizzas, Ellie realizes in dismay that they have forgotten after all to order one for the homeless man, and tries to get her group to donate him a piece each, which all but one is willing to do. Ironically, however, when they go out again, Ellie carrying the saved pizza slices, he has disappeared, his spot vacated and 'the road a dark vacuum, sweeping towards Chinatown'.

Now there is so much about this story that verifiably conforms to the details of a real-life incident in which I was involved, that even I, with all of the views about fiction I express above, tended to think of it as a 'found' story, which is perhaps why, unusually for me, I instinctively kept the real-life names of the pizza takeaway and the road (which in turn perhaps led the magazine editor, who was familiar with my other work, to ask if it were indeed the truth). I was indeed out on the town with a group of friends: we'd been to a poetry reading where the wine had flowed freely, and like the gang of friends in the story we were all a bit drunk. And my friend who shall remain nameless did indeed, like Ellie in the story, lead us all off for a pizza and then remember she had no money and with drunken irony ask a guy begging outside the pizza place to lend her some. And he did respond in a good-natured, matter-of-fact way—basically, they hit it off, really; they seemed to like and understand each other in an instant. She did ask him about his situation: she asked him where he spent the night, and he told her Chinatown, just like the guy in the story, and he did wax philosophical about it.

Really, it was just too comically (and movingly) good to be true for a writer, though I must say that, with a few glasses of wine inside me, I wasn't consciously thinking that at the time, I was just hugely entertained and moved. I suspect, though, that it was at this moment, the moment which struck such a chord for me, that my subconscious began plumbing the whole experience for a story and thus shaping it.

There were other events following on from this moment that can be and have been corroborated by others who were present: just like Ellie in the story, our friend did promise that we'd get the homeless man a pizza, and she did then forget, and try and make us all donate a slice of our own pizzas to him; one of us did refuse, and then, ironically, he had disappeared anyway by the time we got outside.

And it's true that there really were three customers in the Babylon with the same appearance and demeanour as those in the story — a gnarled old drunk, a thin thirtyish guy in an old jacket and the nervous-seeming researcher, though of course we must remember that this was only how I *perceived* them. But if there were any other people in the place, apart from the pizza cooks, I simply don't remember, and while this may be a function of the fact that the story has now replaced the reality, I also think it's possibly because by this time during the incident my writing antennae were out (without my knowing it) and my brain was already or very soon afterwards busy making selections.

Crucially, our friend did go up to the researcher and ask him about himself, and some of us — I don't remember how many — did think he said he was researching 'condensed metaphysics'.

Now that was a just wonderful gift — that phrase so fortuitously linking with the philosophical bent of the homeless man. It's this sort of thing — the connections, ideas and images, that distinguish a resonant story from a mere series of events, and it is up to the writer, of course, to notice them, and to keep the antennae out for them. In fact this connection didn't strike me until the following morning as I was waking, and I think a lot of this sort of 'gelling' goes on while we're asleep. I saw then immediately that it could be the focal point, the basis for a story. As soon as I saw that, I saw another connection which could turn it into a complete story: I saw all of us in the pizza parlour—along with the homeless man outside—as a microcosm of society, and this suddenly linked for me with the notion of condensed-matter physics, the subject that the researcher was really studying, both in real life and in the story. Condensed-matter physics is the study of the relationships between the particles of solid matter, and it seems that (at the time of writing the story, at any rate) the issue of what happens to those relationships when outer forces are brought to bear on solid matter has yet to be properly researched. This struck me as a great metaphor for our relationships in society as a whole, for the potential stories of some of the pizza-place inhabitants (the pressures they had undergone in their lives), and for the effect they all had on each other in that one small but potentially significant incident.

So that was it: with the motifs of philosophy/metaphysics and condensed-matter physics joined together in that one phrase *condensed metaphysics*, I was off on a story. This early stage of writing for me is always more instinctual than intellectual; it's a question of 'feeling' what's right rather than thinking logically—though not entirely: some part of my brain will still be coming in with more logical editorial decisions. So this was my state of mind—largely instinctual, but with an undercurrent of critical logic—as I wrote the first draft of the story: pulling in all the things from the previous evening that fitted these concepts of philosophy, the relationships between particles in physical matter, relationships in society, and people's personal histories, eliminating those that didn't fit, and making up others.

I elaborated the homeless man's philosophical speech. He had indeed told us not to worry about him sleeping in Chinatown, and that the Triads were a myth, but, launched on the philosophy theme, I picked up on his unspoken implications and gave him more to say, and more explicitly, about society in general. In reality the 'condensed metaphysics' incident was fairly brief: only two or three of us, as I say, heard the researcher wrongly, or indeed heard him at all, and he corrected us straightaway, and briefly explained, when our friend asked him, what condensed-matter physics was. Out of that moment of misunderstanding I wove something much more complex. In reality, although the old drunk had taken an interest in everyone's pizzas, just as in the story, and the man in the tweed jacket had clearly been watching everything that was going on, neither of them had said very much at all. But I had been very struck (and moved) by the interest taken in everyone else by these two people, both of whom looked as if they were on the edges of society, and I guess that a fundamental part of the writer's task is to be responsive to such things and sense their potential for development. Swept along now on my notion of the ways people relate to each other in society, I brought these two characters, and everyone else including the pizza cooks, into a comical (I hope) discussion about what 'condensed metaphysics' must mean. In the story the drunk becomes a veritable pizza-parlour philosopher, and reveals a backstory, full of the pressures of society, which is my pure invention — or more accurately, probably, pulled from somewhere else in the depths of my subconscious memory store. Propelled by my philosophy theme and the metaphorical notion of solid-matter particles, I made the researcher talk more than he had in real life, and more philosophically, about condensed-matter physics—I rushed off downstairs at that point to check in the physics book where I now remembered I'd once read a bit about it.

There were certain images in my memory of the night before that resonated deeply for me: the way we all moved back and forth in the mirrors around the wall, the pizza cooks tossing the coloured chopped vegetables and the lights of Chinatown which we looked towards when we came out of the takeaway and found the homeless man gone. However, it was only as I was writing these images into the story that I came to see that they were kaleidoscopic images and thus appropriately symbolic of my particle-relationship theme. In fact, I didn't include the lights, because when I came to the end, and the image of the road sweeping towards Chinatown, I knew that what I wanted was an image of blankness and darkness. To refer to the bright lights of Chinatown at the end of the dark sweep, in the place to which the homeless guy had presumably gone, would have cut across this. This was a very logical, conscious editorial decision: by this time, the end of the story, with the mainly instinctual gallop of the first draft behind me, the logical, editing part of my brain was starting to take over. In fact, I reasoned to myself, the lights were not a *truly* kaleidoscopic image in that, unlike the other two images, they were static. (Later, though, I was sorry that the lights were missing from the story—they still *felt* an integral part of it —and when I came to write a short screenplay adaptation I realized that I could not only include them but instruct a camera to make them appear to move kaleidoscopically!) The seemingly weird thing is that I am quite sure that these images were essential, even central, to my experience of the incident before I consciously saw it as a story, which is why I suspect that even inside the experience my brain was already subconsciously turning it into a story and selecting appropriate images.

As for my other friend, the one who decided not to save a piece of pizza for the homeless man: she shall most definitely remain nameless, since in no way did she do it with the bad grace of the character in the story. The character in the story was compelled to do it like that to spoil the convivial atmosphere in the takeaway and thus fulfil my theme of the pressures of society and the way they upset our relationships within it. My friend in reality just thought we were being patronizing, and would have no part in that, and no one else in the takeaway knew anything about it.

But then that just wouldn't have been such a good story.

FAVOURITE SHORT STORIES

'A Conversation with my Father' by Grace Paley from *Enormous Changes at the Last Minute* (Virago, 1979)

'The Universal Story' and 'Gothic' by Ali Smith from *The Whole Story and Other Stories* (Hamish Hamilton, 2003)

'After the Quake' by Haruki Murakami (The Harvill Press, 2002)

'Ignathous' by Matthew Licht from *The Moose Show* (Salt, 2007)

IDEAS FOR FURTHER EXPLORATION

ONE

This is an exercise for two or more people. Go together to a café (it's best for this exercise that you both experience very similar things). Afterwards write about it. (Your piece doesn't need to be a proper story, but you may find it turns into one.) Meet up and compare your accounts. Discuss the implications: how differently did you each perceive things, and in what ways were you shaping the occasion into potential stories?

TWO

This is an exercise exploring the way memory shapes real life into stories. Think of someone you have known for some time, and incidents you shared—a relative is good! Ask them if they remember one of these incidents (if they say no, ask about others until they say yes!) but—and this is important—*try to avoid discussing the incident.* Go away and write about it. Now ask them what they remember about the incident. Consider the similarities and differences in your accounts, and the implications for storytelling.

THREE

A classic exercise—and time-honoured writer's trick—is to listen in to the conversations of strangers when you're waiting at bus stops or in queues etc, where endless stories are offered up for the taking, tantalizingly incomplete with plenty of scope for authorial shaping. A good way of increasing your own scope with such stories is to stand somewhere where crowds can pass you and listen out for snippets, treating them as writers' prompts.

FOUR

Another classic is to take a newspaper account and write the fleshed-out story behind it. An interesting exercise is to do this with a story which is reported in great detail, and then with another which is only briefly mentioned in the newspaper. What was the difference between the two writing experiences? Which was easier? Which was most fulfilling, and why?

TANIA HERSHMAN

ART BREATHES FROM CONTAINMENT:
THE DELIGHTS OF THE SHORTEST FICTION
OR
THE VERY SHORT STORY THAT COULD

'Let there be light.' What an economy of words, in one of the oldest stories in existence! A more verbose pen might have spun this into: 'Let it be that a glowing and bountiful light shineth down upon the heavens and the earth.' Seventeen words. Seventeen words which add nothing to the perfect, four-word instruction.

So it is with flash fiction, also called short shorts or prose poetry. If a short story is loosely defined as a piece of writing where every word counts, whose length is no more and no less than the story deserves—as opposed to a novella or novel where there are a minimum of pages that must be filled to satisfy the genre—flash fiction takes this to the extreme: no comma, no space, no paragraph break is thoughtlessly entered.

There is no lower limit here: flash fiction is a story distilled to its very essence, the strongest and most potent heart of the tale. And this strength and potency is obtained through what is *not* included, rather than what is. In a flash story of 50 words or 750 words, reading between the lines is imperative.

In the short story 'Segue', from her *Collected Stories,* Carol Shields' main character describes beautifully what a sonnet (whose literal translation is 'little sound') means to her, and I would like to steal this and claim it as a perfect definition of flash fiction:

> a little sound, a ping in the great wide silent world, . . . a splash of noise but a carefully measured splash that is saved from preciosity by the fact that it comes from within the body's own borders; one voice, one small note extended, and then bent; the bending is everything . . . From there, the 'little sound' sparks and forms itself out of the dramatic contrasts of private light and darkness.

Flash fiction, this 'one small note extended', is not something dreamed up by the 21st century purveyors of *fast* everything, to fit onto tiny hand-held screens or to appeal to ever-shrinking attention spans. The masters of short fiction — Borges, Kafka, Raymond Carver, Margaret Atwood and many others — wrote and continue to write short short stories. In fact, as with the best short stories and poetry, flash fiction requires great attention, otherwise the potency is missed, otherwise it's nothing more than a small bundle of words.

The most powerful fiction, the writing that leaves an indelible impression, makes demands upon the reader; reading it is not a passive process. Whether novel, poetry, or short story, such writing engages your imagination, lures you into its world and demands that the characters and scenarios come alive inside your head. Of course, there are many readers who don't want to do this work, who prefer to sit back and watch the story unfold without any effort. However, for the reader looking to be taken on a brief, intense and magical journey, there is no match for great flash fiction.

Take, for example, Grace Paley's story, 'Justice — A Beginning', from *Flash Fiction Forward*, an anthology of very short stories, edited by James Thomas and Robert Shapard. In its scant two pages, it moves, to borrow Paley's character Faith's own words, from 'daily fact to planetary metaphor'. Faith has just finished jury duty during which, 'as a member of the general worldwide mother's union', she had watched the mother of the suspect, who had robbed a grocer at gunpoint: '. . . Faith thought as she often did of the great gun held at the world's head and of the cheaper guns pointing every which way at all the little nations that had barely gotten their heads up.'

On her way home, Faith notices that a building has been torn down and has a short conversation with a stranger about deterioration. When she gets home — at the beginning of the second page — her son Anthony is there with his girlfriend. Faith goes to her room to rest:

> After about an hour Anthony knocked on the door. Ma, when you're finished being private, come out and have some tea with us. We have some bad news for you. This wasn't true, but if he said, Let's have some tea and pie, we

have some wonderful news for you, she'd never leave her room.

Okay, she said, coming to the door. I'm ready, I guess. For God's sake, tell me.

This is where the story ends. It has been no more than an hour or two of Faith's life, and a few minutes of our time. We learn about her attitude towards the justice system, her sympathy for mothers, her concern that the world around her is crumbling, her relationship with her son, her terrible fear that the worst is going to happen. Faith is real to us. She is no paper cut-out. We hear and see her from the first paragraph. And although the end of the story does not tie anything neatly up for us, this doesn't leave us dissatisfied. We have been given enough.

Paley does not do this, as some might imagine, by moving at a rapid pace, by running through as many events as possible as if this were a sprint rather than a marathon. The sense is not of a writer rushing, skimping. The prose is rich: the guilty man's mother is described as having a face 'like a dying flower in its late-season, lank leafage of yellow hair'. That's thirteen words of description in a story approximately 500 words long. Paley has not felt that a very short story necessitates the absence of description. The flower metaphor is a vital part of this piece and it would be less without it.

What Paley understands is what is needed and what isn't. No preamble for the story she is telling, such as the arrival of the jury duty summons, the details of the jury duty itself, the introduction of Faith's son, details of his girlfriend, the background to their relationship. Had she chosen this route, which of course is perfectly possible, it would have become an entirely different story. Paley's story is this length deliberately and composed of these elements only to suit the purpose for which she intended it.

Another piece from *Flash Fiction Forward*, 'Words' by John A. McCaffrey, illustrates this just as sharply. It tells the story of a relationship in two pages, a scene that takes place over the course of several minutes, a tiny corner of the canvas which contains within it the entire painting. The protagonist, left alone in his Chinese girlfriend's apartment when she goes out for pizza, finds a notebook containing a list of English words he has spoken to her and their definitions:

> The first one is *possessive*. It is almost scratched into the paper. . . . He mouths the definition: *A desire for ownership, occupancy, hold.* This he connects to her accusation of his infidelity. The second word, *resolve*, is one he has used about his pending divorce. The third is *content*. It is written so faint he has to hold up the page to his eyes to make out the definition: *Happy enough with what one has or is, not desiring something more or different.*

Using this plot device, the finding of the girlfriend's vocabulary list, our protagonist's world opens up before us like a flower in bloom. We have everything we need: about her from the words she has chosen to define; about him from his reactions to the words.

The words are symbolic, they are keys that unlock many doors, and we are allowed to see far enough through each to understand what is going on. Any reader who has had a relationship, or has read about relationships, will follow the shorthand here: this is about intimacy, the violation of it, failures in communication that result not just from linguistic confusion but from something far more basic about human interaction. And this is also a love story. This is particular *and* universal. We read this and nod our heads. Yes, we *get* this, this is known to us.

What do these two stories have in common? One is told in the past tense ('Faith leaned'); the other in the present ('He sees'). One unfolds mostly in a straightforward, linear way, one event happening after another; the other uses flashbacks. One story takes place over several hours and in several different places, the other over a few minutes and in one place. One has a number of characters (Faith, the convicted man's mother, the man in the street, Faith's son, his girlfriend); the other only two (our protagonist and his girlfriend). They are both told in the third person point of view ('he reads', 'Faith walked'), but many of the other stories in the *Flash Fiction Forward* anthology are told in first person ('I spoke').

The only common element these two stories definitively share is *brevity*. Their length is what allows them to be collected under the heading of 'flash fiction'. Apart from that, there is nothing that flash fiction cannot be, there is no prohibition on style, content, tone, pace, setting, point of view, linear or non-linear narrative.

However, in my opinion, flash fiction does lend itself very well to more surreal or 'irreal' stories. Because there is an unspoken contract between writer and reader of flash fiction that the author is going to provide few, if any, details about the world we are being asked to step into, I contend that the reader more willingly accepts oddities and suspends disbelief in the 'truth' of such worlds than with a longer piece. For example, 'Wearing Dad's Head', by Barry Yourgrau, the title story of his collection, simply presents the reader with a small boy who is trying on his father's head. The story ends with the boy and a collection of his friends, all wearing their dads' heads. Yourgrau says nothing by way of explanation about whether in this world one can try on *all* body parts, or what the person whose head has been 'borrowed' does in the meantime! No, he simply offers this to the reader and asks us to follow him for several pages. The reader who takes up the challenge will be well rewarded.

What of writing flash stories? Well, there are two methods by which this may be done: cutting a longer story, or setting out with the aim of writing a very short story.

Paring down a longer story is always a useful exercise: you quickly discover how much is unnecessary, how much is repetition, how much can be shed while still retaining enough meaning, leaving the reader to fill in between the lines. I have had much success in reducing a 2500 story down to 250 words: once you begin, you quickly slice away at the paragraphs you realise were unnecessarily bloated, wondering how you could ever have thought that all these words were needed. However, this method is not unique to flash, it can — and should — equally be applied to longer works. A good writer always has to engage in the slash-and-burn!

Deliberately setting out to write a 500-word or 50 word first draft is a different matter. Limitation is good for the creative process, says Carol Shields in her short story, 'Segue', as her main character sits down to write her sonnet:

> [T]hink of Leonardo and his sage wisdom; 'Art breathes from containment and suffocates from freedom'. Or the problems that accrue from the 'weight of too much liberty' (Wordsworth) . . . . Think of that rectangle, perfect in its proportions, that plastic cutlery tray in your kitchen drawer, with its sharp divisions for forks, knives, spoons.

> Or think of the shape of a human life which, like it or not,
> is limited.

In 'Segue', the poet writes the 14 lines of the sonnet over as many days, which is another way to approach very short stories, writing them slowly, weighing up each word, each line.

However, the technique I would like to recommend is as *flash* as the end product! Set aside twenty or thirty minutes of time (or less as you become more practised). An alarm clock is useful if you don't want to keep checking your watch. You are going to write with the awareness at the back of your mind that at the end of this time you will wrap up and come to an end. You are going to write *knowing* that after twenty or thirty minutes you will have a complete flash story.

You may already, as often happens, have a first sentence or an idea that has been floating around in your head for some time, begging to be written down. Or you may have faith that as soon as your time begins, you will pluck an idea from the air and begin to write.

If, as is frequently the case for me, you need some stimuli, reach for several books, or search for short stories or poetry on the Internet, and 'borrow' six or seven words and phrases from different works to create a set of 'prompts'. (I prefer poetry for this purpose, because of the poet's talent for pairing unlikely words, which tends to set my imagination spiralling in interesting directions!) If you do this in advance of your writing session, try not to dwell too much on the prompts you have chosen, so that you can come to them fresh when you begin to write.

When the allotted time begins, take a minute or two to read through the prompts, and then, when one of them sparks something in you, begin to write, slipping this word or phrase into your story. Whenever you sense that you need a little more stimulation, reach for another prompt, insert it, and allow it to take you along new paths. Anything goes here. Try and use all the prompts, but don't worry if you don't manage to!

Be aware of the time passing and the need to be working towards an ending. Start *closing in* your story rather than adding tendrils that could open it out into new plot twists, new characters. When the time is up, stop writing. You have just written your first flash story!

Endings are the parts of flash fiction that I find I most often have to edit. All writers have a tendency to want to wrap things up neatly, tie up all loose ends. In other words: we keep writing long after we should have stopped. One of my teachers advised that we always cut the final paragraph of a story, it is almost always too much. With a flash story, it is more likely to be a line or two, but this is not something to be concerned with at the time of writing. That comes later, when you can look at your story more objectively, after a few weeks or months. Often it will be an astute editor who, when accepting your flash story for publication, will suggest edits that you yourself couldn't see.

As I have said, this 'blast' method of writing flash fiction takes practice. As you do it more and more, you learn how to pace your story so that it does begin and end within your allotted time, reining in the impulse to make the story 'bigger'.

There are those who may later take a flash story they have written and use it as the basis for a longer story, which is, of course, permitted. Nothing is forbidden! However, I want to stress that this flash writing is not an *exercise*, it is not a *warm-up* to writing something longer, to get the fingers moving. These flash stories are not sketches as you work up to the 'real thing'. It *is* the real thing. There is an end product, one which the market is becoming more and more interested in publishing.

Another benefit to writing an entire flash story in such a short time is that it is something that can be done often, and therefore the file of stories you have written becomes satisfyingly larger and larger. This both exercises the writing *muscle*—I am a great believer in this concept: the more you write, the more you will write—and it also has the side-effect that you are less attached to each individual piece, it is not your most precious and solitary offspring, so if you write one or two stories you are not so pleased with, tomorrow is another day!

As I mentioned, there is an increasing number of literary journals, both in print and online, eager to read your flash stories, from 50 words and upwards, and many readers who are willing to be your audience. The Internet is an excellent medium for flash fiction because it is easier to read on the screen than a longer story that requires much scrolling down. There are also many small presses publishing chapbooks of flash fiction, often beautifully hand-printed, in the same way that poetry chapbooks have been produced for many years. And the contests for flash fiction often offer a large financial reward per word submitted!

I will end with a health warning: flash fiction (reading and writing it) can be addictive. A two-page story as astonishing, sharp and essential as those I mentioned above shakes the system. The heart pounds, each word carries weight and density, each sentence is many-layered. This is due to the writers' skill, but also because the reader knows when beginning the story that this will all be over when the page is turned, that you will be immersed in this world for only the blink of an eye. The demand made of the writer in these few pages is sky-high: wow me, move me, *change* me.

When you see what can be done in such a limited space, you will wonder why short stories, novellas and novels don't adhere to the same economy of words, with each word carrying so much charge? If only all of life could be this concise, this intense!

 REFERENCE BOOKS

Collected Short Stories by Carol Shields (Harper Perennial, 2005)
Flash Fiction Forwards Eds: J Thomas and R Shapard (WW Norton, 2006)
Wearing Dad's Head by Barry Yourgrau (Arcade, 1999)

 FAVOURITE SHORT STORIES

'Wait' by Roy Kesey from *All Over* (Dzanc Books, 2007)
'Speak to Me' by Paddy O'Reilly from *The End of the World* (University of Queensland Press, 2007)
'God's Gift' by Ali Smith from *Other Stories and Other Stories* (Penguin, 2004)
'The One with the Bullet' by Tobias Wolff from *The Night In Question* (Vintage, 1997)
'Runaway' by Alice Munro from *Runaway* (Knopf, 2004)
'Bravado' by William Trevor from *Cheating at Canasta* (Viking, 2007)
'Dearth' by Aimee Bender from *Willful Creatures* (Anchor Books, 2006)
'Squeak, Memory' by Melvin J Bukiet from *A Faker's Dozen* (WW Norton, 2003)

IDEAS FOR FURTHER EXPLORATION

From Tania Hershman's essay:

Reach for several books, or search for short stories or poetry on the internet, and 'borrow' six or seven phrases—of two words or more—from different works to create a set of 'prompts' (I prefer poetry for this purpose, because of the poet's talent for pairing unlikely words, which tends to set my imagination spiralling in interesting directions!). If you do this in advance of your writing session, try not to dwell too much on the prompts you have chosen, so that you can come to them fresh when you begin to write. Set yourself 20 minutes to write in. Take a minute or two to read through the prompts, and then, when one of them sparks something in you, begin to write, slipping this word or phrase into your story. Whenever you feel stuck, reach for another prompt, insert it, and allow it to take you along new paths. Anything goes here. Try and use all the prompts, but don't worry if you don't manage to! Be aware of the time passing and the need to be working towards an ending. Start closing in your story rather than adding tendrils that could open it out into new plot twists, new characters. When the time is up, stop writing.

DAVID GAFFNEY

GET SHORTY: THE MICRO FICTION OF ETGAR KERET

Ernest Hemingway once said his best work was a story he wrote in just six words:

For sale: baby shoes, never worn.

I'm not sure that's a short story but the writer I'm going to talk about, Etgar Keret, an Israeli who's published three collections of short-short stories, writes very, very short pieces of text you would probably describe as 'micro' or 'flash' fiction — stories usually of less than 500 words, and often as short as 100.

There's a lot to learn from authors who've mastered this ultra short form — precision, efficiency, economy of language — and Etgar Keret demonstrates that in a couple of pages you can have everything; a beginning, a middle, an end, character development, and descriptions; all the qualities of a longer story contained in a tiny Polly Pocket world.

The two-page story, 'Drops', from Keret's 2006 collection *Missing Kissinger*, begins by dropping us right into the thick of one of Keret's peculiar worlds:

> My girlfriend says someone in America invented a medi-
> cine against feeling alone.

The narrator's girlfriend heard about the magical medicine that cures loneliness on a programme (we don't know if it's radio or TV because you don't get much information in the world of micro fiction) called *Nightline* and she sent off right away. The medicine comes in two forms — drops or spray can, and she opted for drops, which you put in your ear.

You might ask of this story — who are these people? Where are they? What do they look like? But we don't know any of these facts. And this brings us to the first golden rule of micro fiction — DON'T USE TOO MANY CHARACTERS. You often don't have time to describe your characters when you're writing ultra short. Even a name may not be useful in a micro story unless it conveys a lot of additional story-information or saves you words elsewhere.

You will also notice that 'Drops', like most of Keret's stories, is written from a first person point of view, and many micro stories avoid third person narration. In a world with no names, the 'I' is useful because you can easily have two other characters — he and she — without the need for names.

At first glance there doesn't seem to be a lot of information in the first paragraph of 'Drops', but we can guess a lot about the world and the people featured in the story from the few clues Keret leaves lying around in his spare text; the narrator is in a city, people are lonely, the world seems fragmented, nobody is connecting with anyone else, and someone has invented a medicinal cure for loneliness rather than finding a way to get people together. We know from the name of the programme she refers to — *Nightline* — that it's probably a late night phone-in show which would appeal to a lonely listenership; insomniacs, shiftworkers, unemployed, sick and disabled, and we recognise a market segment which some cynical advertising agency has identified as ripe for exploitation. And Keret, in grand micro-fiction style, gives us all of this information just in the title of the programme, leaving us suspecting that these 'loneliness drops' are modern day X-ray specs or space-monkeys.

We are then told that the nameless narrator of 'Drops' has an unhappy girlfriend who is suspicious that he is cheating on her. She believes that these loneliness-curing drops will allow her to leave him and live alone with no negative consequences.

> No stinking eardrops are going to love you the way I love you, he tells her. Except that eardrops won't cheat on her either, she says and then she leaves.

Here, Keret illustrates the second golden rule of writing micro fiction—START IN THE MIDDLE. You don't have time in this very short form to set scenes and build up character. Within the first two sentences of 'Drops' there's a lot of information to take in: a failing relationship, a world where loneliness can be solved by some occult medical process, and a woman who would rather opt for a medical prevention of loneliness than live with the emotionally stunted partner she suspects of cheating.

You will also notice in 'Drops' that rather than build suspense —will the drops arrive? Will they work? Will she stay or will she go?—the girlfriend has left him by the end of sentence two and we hear no more about the drops. We are now left with the narrator alone and may wonder what is left to tell of this weird story.

This brings us to the third golden rule of micro fiction—MAKE SURE THE ENDING ISN'T AT THE END. One of the big disadvantages of micro stories is that you are in and out of the fictional world too quickly—these slivers of fiction don't allow the reader time to absorb ideas. In micro fiction there's a danger that much of the engagement with the story takes place when the reader has stopped reading. To avoid this, Keret places the denouement in the middle of the story, allowing us time, as the rest of the text spins out, to consider the situation along with the narrator, and ruminate on the decisions his characters have taken. Placing the end in the middle is a useful technique. If you're not careful, micro stories can lean towards punch line based or 'pull back to reveal' endings which have a one-note, gag-a-minute feel. Micro fiction isn't good at fading out and can tend towards the drum roll and cymbal crash. In 'Drops', Keret avoids this by giving us almost all the information we need to understand the story and the characters in the first few lines, allowing him to use the last few paragraphs to take us on a journey below the surface, which he does by describing how the narrator is feeling now he is left alone. The narrator doesn't have any friends who would send him drops to cure loneliness but if he did have friends:

> I would go drinking with them tell them my troubles and hug them a lot. I wouldn't be embarrassed to cry next to them and stuff.

A little reverse-engineering leads us to the possible seed of Keret's premise—that people are driven to relationships by a fear of loneliness and that if we conquer this fear maybe we can all be happier and live alone? But a premise is not a story and Keret makes a story out of it, and one of the ways he adds resonance to the story is by his title, which is the fourth golden rule of micro fiction—SWEAT YOUR TITLE, make it work for a living.

Keret would have had many options for a method to deliver his anti-loneliness drug — pills, injections, syrups — but he chooses drops, a quaint, almost medieval way of ingesting a drug. The title also makes us think of teardrops, of dropping out of the world, of a descent into something, even the hangman's drop. Then Keret ends the story by emphasising how happy the narrator would be if he had those friends to hug and cry in front of:

we could spend years that way, our whole life. A hundred per cent natural, much better than drops.

. . . and here comes the fifth golden rule — MAKE YOUR LAST LINE RING LIKE A BELL. The last line is not the ending — we had that in the middle remember — but it should leave the reader with something which will continue to sound after the story has finished. It should not complete the story but rather take us into a new place, a place where we can continue to think about the ideas in the story, puzzle over them, and wonder what it all meant. A story that gives itself up in the last line is no story at all, and after reading a piece of good micro fiction, we should be struggling to understand it and, in this way, will grow to love it as a beautiful enigma. And this is also another one of the dangers of micro fiction: micro stories can be too rich and offer too much emotion in a powerful one-off injection, overwhelming the reader, flooding the mind. A few micro shorts now and again will amaze and delight — one after another and you feel like you've been run over by lorry full of fridges.

Micro stories are nimble, nippy little things that can park on a sixpence and accelerate quickly away and they may look quick and easy to write — but they're not. It takes a lot of work to do what Etgar Keret does. The last golden rule of micro fiction is

WRITE LONG, THEN GO SHORT — create a lump of stone from which you chip out your story sculpture. Worried about reducing your glittering prose to a bloody stump? Well don't be. Stories can live much more cheaply than you realise, with little deterioration in lifestyle. Editing your stories down to this distilled perfection can be like demolishing a building from the inside, but as 'Drops' shows, Keret is a master. His tiny stories have a formal and emotional exactness and in reading them you find yourself lost in Keret's frozen little shards of time, and you hold your breath, suspended between an endless known moment and an endless unknown future. But beware: writing micro fiction is, for some, like holidaying in a caravan — the grill may well fold out to become an extra bed, but you wouldn't sleep in a fold down grill for the rest of your life.

This article was previously published by Tindal Street Press in association with the *Birmingham Post*.

 ## FAVOURITE SHORT STORIES

Examples of flash fiction worth looking at, and representing a range of styles are:

'The World's Greatest Impressionist' by David Bateman on The Phone Book: www.the-phone-book.com

'These Certain Young People' by Dave Eggers on Guardian Online: www.guardian.co.uk

'Lipstick' by Dan Rhodes from *Anthropology and a Hundred Other Stories* (Canongate, 2005)

'The Lost Tree' by Richard Brautigan on his website: www.brautigan.net

'My Guardian Angel' from *The World Doesn't End* by Charles Simic (Harvest Books, 1989)

 # IDEAS FOR FURTHER EXPLORATION

ONE

Last Lines: Remove the last line from a story. Can you replace it?

TWO

Reducing text: Reduce this paragraph as much as you can. It's 169 words long—aim for at least half that:

> It was necessary to rekindle the love in our marriage so we decided to go back to where we spent our honeymoon, Crete. We would stay in the same hotel, eat in the same restaurants, lie on the same beaches, do everything like we did thirty years ago. We were sure that if we did those things then our relationship would return to normal and we would fall in love with each other again.
>
> It was surprising how little had changed in the village. On the first night we went to our old favourite restaurant, Paloukis, sat down at virtually the same table we'd sat at 30 years ago, and ordered virtually the same dishes. But someone had sucked the soul out of Paloukis. Helen

suspected that the business had been sold to some outsider, gobbled up by some soulless chain, whereas as I deduced that the owner had probably just retired and passed it on to his son.

(from *Sawn-off Tales* by David Gaffney, Salt 2006)

THREE

Titles: Come up with a title for the following story:

The sorting hall was said to be a special dept where people with no useful function were sent. No-one knew if it really existed. One lunchtime he scoured industry house, from the rooftop to the basement, looking for it. He saw suited executives nibbling biscuits, girls tapping at computers, men at drawing boards, and, in a room marked training, a group building a structure with toilet-roll holders. But there was no trace of the sorting hall.

Back at his desk they had already brought the afternoon's bins. He looked forward to examining the contents as there was always something exciting. He began to classify, measure and catalogue. A tissue, which he placed in a twizzle bag and labelled. A crumpled A4 sheet to be smoothed out and placed in a file. A crisp packet.

He enjoyed his job. He would leave industry house altogether if anything ever changed.

(from *Sawn-off Tales* by David Gaffney, Salt 2006)

MARIAN GARVEY

ON INTUITION: WRITING INTO THE VOID

I once met a man whose birthday it was, and I sent him a bouquet of flowers. 'If he's an Irishman, I'm telling ye,' my mother said, 'he'll run.' And in my speech at our wedding, later that year, I said, 'Yes Mum, in the right direction!'.

I reveal these differing attitudes to 'courtship', as my mother calls it, because mother and daughter represent the split we have in us as writers. One is based on intuition, the other on direction, though perhaps that might more accurately be phrased as: the desperation to know what direction we are moving in.

Rew defines intuition as 'knowledge of a fact or truth, as a whole; immediate possession of knowledge independent of linear reasoning process'.

In the story of the man and the flowers, my mother would say I had definitely acted independently of 'the linear reasoning process'. And she was right. Sending the flowers was a hunch. I 'just knew' it was the right thing to do.

Clinical nurse practitioners, Rovithis and Parissopoulos, in their study on how intuition is an integral part of nursing care, give an example of how life-saving intuition can be. They recount the example of the A&E nurse who sent for the cardiac arrest team even though her patient, whilst sweating and pale, was displaying perfectly normal vital signs on the cardiac monitor. The man proceeded to have a cardiac arrest, though fortunately the medical team were at hand and able to save him. The nurse described 'a gut feeling' and along with this and past knowledge of a similar experience and patient cues, she was able to respond instantly, and on some level unconsciously, to the patient's changing situation. This type of 'unconscious sudden analysis of cues, as gaps of data filled into a complete pattern' can be seen to enhance the linear analytical approach to the nursing process. The authors of this paper believe that this type of intuition can not only be valuable to nurse practitioners who use it naturally (often highly skilled and experienced nurses), but that it can also be 'taught' to other nurses. Harnessing intuition. Now there's a thought.

I think that in writing a short story, exactly this has to happen. It might not feel quite like the life and death situation of the A&E Department, but we all recognise a dead story when we see one. All fiction requires an imaginative act. This has to include the moment when gaps are suddenly 'filled into a complete pattern', often long before any writing has begun. What is key, is to listen and follow from this 'knowing', i.e. the suddenly 'familiar', into to the 'unfamiliar'. Within this journey, lies the story.

When Raymond Carver talks about finding the time, literally, to sit down and write a story, the first line of which had been in his head, he talks about how 'the story offered itself to me'. He says he knew a story was there and wanted telling—'I felt it in my bones'. Once he sat down, and put down one line after another, the story emerged 'and I knew it was my story'.

The way he describes the process, it's as if he's discovered it along the way. He's discovered what he already 'knew'. He just didn't know the route/direction he would move in until he got there. Rew's nurses are the same. The nurse with the cardiac patient had a 'gut feeling'. When asked what made her summon the cardiac arrest team she said, 'I just knew it'. For me, when I write a short story, there is this pinprick of sudden knowing at the core, before I've begun. This is not a plan of action. It may be an image, a sound, a sentence, but whatever it is, the act of writing the rest of the story somehow finds me working through the unfamiliar towards the inevitable.

An example of this from my own work was in the Asham award-winning story, 'All That's Left'. In the heat of high summer, two sisters play in the courtyard of their house which is covered with scaffolding. A tin bath of cement has been left by builders who have gone to 'their tea'. The older of the girls strips and submerges herself in the bath of cement, bossily instructing the younger sister to raid their mother's flower beds to plant on top of her. Upstairs, the mother packs their father's clothes in a state of near collapse. The father's absence in the family is palpable. The image I had, was of the older girl sitting on a bench under the honeysuckle watching and contemplating the bath of cement. 'It is the weight that attracts her', the first line of the story, was the sudden 'pinprick', the core. It is the moment when she desires to submerge herself. And all the way through, the girl is comforted by the weight of the cement, with the reader, of course, finding it less than comforting. This story was written in one sitting many years ago whilst my daughter crawled around the building site that was our kitchen at the time. It was only many years later that I remembered: 'Oh yes! My father was a builder'.

I think this is the unconscious part that Flannery O'Connor

refers to in the writing process. It imbues the bath of cement with a meaning and a history which I, as the writer, was not fully aware I was providing. In dance, Richard Alston refers to this as the 'history of the gesture'.

Flannery O'Connor talks of the organic nature of this unravelling. How each story form is unique; that the form cannot be superimposed on the story and that the organic nature of the story will reveal itself. She explains this so clearly in her famous 'Good Country People' story where the Ph.D student has her wooden leg stolen by the travelling Bible salesman. She had no idea this was going to happen until it did happen, shocking herself as the writer, as well as the reader.

She makes the point that, though the story came about 'in a seemingly mindless fashion', there was hardly any rewriting done on it at all. Whilst she says the story was 'under control' in the writing, it was not written entirely consciously, but as she says, 'in a mind-less' fashion. And this is the crux. She refers us to Maritain's 'habit of art' which states that fiction writing is something in which the whole personality takes part—the conscious as well as the unconscious mind. Art, Maritain says is the Artist's habit and needs to be rooted in the whole personality. So we write as we live.

It is this habit of art, this intuition that the writing student needs to cultivate. And O'Connor goes on to say it is more than a discipline, it is a way of seeing, of looking at the world in order that the senses, and that sixth sense of intuition, are able to find as much meaning as possible in things.

This way of being is all very well, but Flannery O'Connor also recognises the practical need for writers to try to improve, to get it right. She and others give advice on keeping images concrete, using the gift of the dialect of the region for example. Melanie

Little urges us to pay attention. All of these 'how-tos' should not be confused with the pursuit of direction.

Knowing what direction you're going in with a story is surely a good thing. With a mother like mine, that can also be said of 'courtship'. Direction can seem purposeful and liberate the writer. After all, direction gives structure but rushing into 'a direction' can force the form of the story before it is ready. It can be terribly seductive up to a point, especially in the hands of a skilful writer but in the end, the story sits on the page. It is reduced by the 'beginning middle and end-ness' of it. It doesn't expand. It becomes an 'act-as-if'. It is not true. When you write a story like this you don't move anywhere, you pretend. You don't transcend what Graham Swift calls the 'fixity, our isolation'. Instead, you fall into the void you are desperately trying to avoid. As Beckett did when he walked the River Liffey, staring into its depths, we have to make the decision to write, to tune in to what we 'know'. We have to write into the void.

If we fill up our stories with every technique available, on one level, we might not get found out for a very long time, because we can be so very good at it. But take a minute and remember. Remember those stories you've read when you're sitting up in bed and you've just finished the book which lies open on your chest, across your heart. Remember its effect? Or in the same bed, another night, another volume. You've closed the book. 'Yeah,' you say to yourself, 'yeah it was . . . good, yeah', and you sigh, not quite getting what it is you're not satisfied with, as you lean over to place it on the bedside table. Then you turn off the light and know in the settling dark that quiet emptiness.

When we read and enter into the world of a story with its characters and their lives, as readers, we can get this moment, as Graham Swift says, when we recognise the familiar but unfamiliar—the 'I've-been-here-too territory' as he calls it, and it's this sense of identification which he calls the 'heartland of fiction, the real destination of story telling'.

How to get to this heartland? How to get the story to go somewhere? You have to be prepared to involve yourself fully, says Graham Swift, to undergo a sort of inner uprooting. 'To become, with all its freedom, risk and excitement, unattached.'

 REFERENCE BOOKS

Intuition, Concept Analysis of a Group Phenomenon by L. Rew (Advances in Nursing Science, 1986)

Intuition in Nursing Practice by Rovithis and Parissopoulos (ICSUS Nurse Web Journal 22, 2005)

Art and Scholasticism and other Essays by Jacques Maritain (FQ Classics 2007)

Complete Stories by Flannery O'Connor (Faber and Faber, 2009)

 FAVOURITE SHORT STORIES

'The Piano Tuner's Wives' by William Trevor from *The Collected Stories* (Penguin, 1993)

'A Small Good Thing' by Raymond Carver from *Where I'm Calling From: The Selected Stories* (Atlantic Monthly Press, 1988)

'Cathedral' by Raymond Carver from *Where I'm Calling From: The Selected Stories* (Atlantic Monthly Press, 1988)

'Slog's Dad' by David Almond from *The National Short Story Prize* (Atlantic Books, 2007)

'What we Talk About When we Talk About Love' by Raymond
    Carver from *Where I'm Calling From: The Selected Stories*
    (Atlantic Monthly Press, 1988)
'Little Lady and a Dog' by Anton Chekov from *Little Lady and a Dog
    and Other Stories, 1896-1904* (Penguin Classics, 2002)
'Teresa's Wedding' by William Trevor from *The Collected Stories*
    (Penguin, 1993)

 IDEAS FOR FURTHER EXPLORATION

Imagine . . .

Take these scenarios and with your means of writing to hand,
read them through slowly, allowing yourself to sink into the
scene. And as you finish the last sentence in each case, begin to
write. Try not to think about it, just write and see what comes.

SKIN

You are in your own bathroom, enjoying a warm bath. The room
is full of steam. You are relaxed, thinking about nothing in particular. Enjoy this sense of relaxation for a few moments, see if you
can feel the warmth of the water, hear the sounds as you move
your hands.

Now imagine you are getting out of the bath and wrapping
yourself in a warm towel. You walk towards the door where you
have hung your clothes on a hook, but instead you see something
else is hanging there.

A skin. A complete skin hanging there. You have no idea who
this might be.

Raising your hands to the back of your neck, you find a fastening you have never noticed before, and are able, quite safely, to unzip your own skin.

Imagine doing so, and then imagine taking the skin hanging on the back of your door, and putting that on instead.

Wait for a moment while you get used to this new sensation. And now cross to the mirror and look at yourself.

And go and write.

RAINBOW

It has been raining. The rain has stopped and the sun is trying to come out, all is brighter, cleaner. Imagine you are going for a walk in the countryside, smelling the scents after rain, feeling the still-wet grass brushing your legs as you pass. Imagine the colours of the fields round you, the different greens of the grass as the clouds and the sun throw shadows across your path.

Suddenly, up ahead of you, hanging over the trees, is a rainbow, a perfect arc, all the colours clear. You walk towards the trees. And see a second rainbow, the colours mirroring the first. A double rainbow hanging in the air.

You walk closer, until the ground rises, and you walk through the trees, up a hill. You glimpse the rainbows as you go, still there above the trees. And, coming out at the top of the hill, you are not only above the trees, spread out below you like a thick carpet, but the rainbows are only just above your head.

You reach up and touch one colour. Just one.

Now go and write.

(with thanks to writer, teacher and editor Zoe King for these exercises)

ELAINE CHIEW

ENDINGS

OPEN CLOSURE

There's a weird parallel in being asked to ponder the nature of endings in fiction as my mother-in-law lay in intensive care at Chelsea Westminster. Given the gravity of her symptoms, we had an inkling that death was round the corner. Our hearts fought the logic and facts. Our hearts went to a cold, cold war with our minds. Yet, the more she faded, the more we hoped.

On a tertiary level, might not some of the best endings in short stories have this effect? You suspect how it's going to end, but you aren't 100% sure; regardless, you're totally engaged—heart, mind, sense. That sense of narrative expectation and engagement, retaining a degree of mystery or openness where the reader may hope or wonder or accept a different ending, tells me the ending is well-earned, the story has been crafted so wonderfully it brings the story to this point I call 'open closure'.

I'm a strong advocate of 'open closure' in short stories. Those with neatly-tied up endings, everything resolved, often seem contrived by the author to me, smacking too much of the 'fairy-tale'. Short stories, by definition, are windows, perhaps a series of windows, a short chunk of life in motion, usually an extraordinary, compelling, or dramatically resonant stroboscopic snapshot of one or a few characters' lives. As such, their endings are a different category of animal than novels. Chekhov, so-called the father of the modern short story, often wrote stories that 'did not end', as Nabokov explained, 'for as long as people are alive, there is no possible and definite conclusion to their troubles or hopes or dreams'. Indeed, there's a sense that life carries on for these characters after our visit with them, that the story is so real it lives beyond its pages.

To achieve this, I believe an ending has to be organic, meaning *it grows out of all that came before*. Antonya Nelson talks about the 'shape of a story' — it is not plot, it is in fact, something other than plot. If one were to visualize the 'shape' of a good short story, one might say it's like a fish. It starts at the mouth and expands upwards in rising actions, like an oval, reaching its climax and denouement, and then it arrives at the tail — the ending, where a twist is possible. Interestingly, the bottom part of the oval, characterized by broken lines, is the part of the story that happens in the reader's mind, the part that lives on, where the total is more than the sum of its parts.

That's not the only 'shape' of a short story, mind you (the 'inverted checkmark' is also common), but it's one that characterizes some of the best stories I've read. This is a helpful image for me, as I write my own, because it emphasizes that the ending is very much part of the whole. It's not just an afterthought or exit punctuation or worse, explanations (e.g. the preachy ending of O'Henry's 'Gift of the Magi' (a great story in its time); today though, a tendency to explain story significance can be a mark of amateurishness).

Everything that comes before dictates the ending. I can't reach my ending without fully contemplating my plot. Nor can I do so without knowing what the story is about—its dramatic heart, its theme being explored, its central conflict, the search of my protagonist, his or her yearning. All very sensible, you say, but what does it mean when I sit down to write? For one thing, it means you can't plan your ending. I believe your ending *finds* you. Especially if you're deep, deep, 20,000 leagues, in your story and character.

This is not as hippy-touchy-feely or lazy as it sounds. There's a whole lot of work that has to be done *on everything else that comes before*, and it's remarkably hard work to let go of wanting to control the ending. To be honest, you're probably better off spending time worrying about all the other story elements—the most important of which is the character—and you could do worse than letting the character take over.

THE EPIPHANY ENDING

There's a trend towards the 'epiphany' ending in modern short fiction. The 'literary epiphany' is contradistinct from its religious meaning (the visit of the Magi), and rather, has to do with the sudden or dawning change upon or realizations of *inner truth* for a protagonist based on the events of the story. Charles Baxter, in his essays on fiction in *Burning Down The House*, noted the rise of the use of this unveiling mechanism in modern short fiction. 'The logic of unveiling has become a dominant mode in Anglo-American writing . . . The loss of innocence, and the arrival of knowingness can become an addiction. Cultures with a fascination with innocence often cannot get enough of these moments.' He went on to reproach its overuse—the 'staleness' and 'rottenness' of these types of climactic revelations. 'Everywhere there is a glut of epiphanies . . . But some of the insights have seemed disturbingly untrustworthy.' Chris Offutt, in an essay called 'Getting It Straight', told how an MFA workshop was spent examining whether an epiphany experienced by a fictional character was effective, earned, and inevitable.

I don't disparage 'epiphany' endings, and I've certainly written my fair share of them, but I do think the automatic application of 'suddenly, I realized' to the ending of a story, with the writer then inserting the relevant epiphanic 'little disturbances' in the character's head, can do a story no service. Moreover, how similar is this to real life really? How often, after being beset by a number of inciting events in our own lives, do we actually arrive at startling, life-changing insights such as our characters seem to do? In my own life, the 'great truths' I begin to grasp about, say, the death of my father—which completely devastated me at the time it happened—are only beginning to reveal itself to me ten years later, with the death of my mother.

Charles Baxter pointed out another interesting thing about 'epiphanies' as endings. They usually have a 'stop-time' effect. The character is challenged by a parting image and reflects inwards, and the spotlight falls on him as the light dims in his surroundings. This is the moment of 'conversion'. There, the story ends. In real life, do your epiphanies not change your subsequent expressed viewpoints and actions? Sure they do. Yet, when the epiphany is used as an ending, we never get to see these changes wrought on our fictional characters. As a reader, we're expected to guess.

I'm not advocating the death of epiphany endings, because I too seek to derive meaning and understanding and knowledge from the short fiction I read and write, and without the 'epiphany' endings, we might be left with very little indeed. However, I do think it could be done with more reflection. Lorrie Moore is brilliant in sprinkling lots of little epiphanies along the way as a story unfolds. She doesn't always rely on the last big bang of insight to conclude a story. Some classic examples of her style are these: *Which Is More Than You Can Say About Some People*, *Community Life* and *People Like That Are The Only People Here*.

In fact, in *People Like That Are The Only People Here*, a major epiphany occurs to the mother, the main character, when her baby is diagnosed with Wilm's tumor, on page 4:

> The mother has begun to cry: all of life has led her here, to this moment. After this, there is no more life. There is something else, something stumbling, something for robots, but not life. Life has been taken and broken, quickly like a stick.

That this epiphany is a bloodshed moment is clear. Does it mean it's true? That life really does end for the mother? Of course not. But it feels true to the mother. It is what she feels. There's a subjective truth in it, which we bow to, but it also reinforces something else that's true about epiphanies—not all of them reflect a universal humanistic truth that's true for all of us. In fact, the epiphanic realization can be as wrong as donkey's logic. And yet, the mother here has perforated into the realm of something true, that others in her situation will no doubt feel, i.e. that her life has been broken in some way.

A couple of pages later, the mother experiences another plangent epiphany:

> You turn just slightly and there it is: the death of your child. It is part symbol, part devil, completely upon you. Then it is a fierce little country abducting you; it holds you squarely inside itself like a cellar room—the best boundaries of you are the boundaries of it. Are there windows? Sometimes aren't there windows?

What Lorrie Moore has done here is to invest in *epiphanic footprints* along the story's meandering path. By doing so, she shows how the mother changes thought and speech as a consequence, the dribble-down effect of a life-altering realization. By doing so, she builds and builds upon the edifice of meaning she's handing us about a mother struggling with the fact of her baby's cancer. By doing so, she does not leave the major epiphany to the ending alone, where the narrative pressure has gathered fit to combust, potentially hobbling much of what came before. Instead of the umpteen stories written with a widespread, humorless, bloodless competence decried by Salman Rushdie in his preface of the 2008 Best American Short Stories, perhaps we'll have less mechanical, less constructed stories. If we let our epiphanies happen along the way, rather than saving them for the end, maybe we'll have a richer, deeper, more profound pyramid of 'revelations', one that's true to the character itself?

Experiencing my father's death in my twenties immunized me against my mother's years later. And with that, came terrible guilt at my inability to feel the enormity of grief I'd felt for my father. If this had been the ending of a short story, how much satisfaction would it have given? Would you rather not hear the story of how this guilt plays out in my life?

TWIST VERSUS SURPRISE

What about the ending with a 'twist'? What about the surprising ending? And what about those stories that start out with the ending in mind, and you work backwards to form the story?

At the risk of sounding controversial, I will say I'm not sure working backwards from an ending you have in mind will result in a good story. Very possibly, you might find what you thought was an ending was actually the beginning.

Endings with a 'twist' are so overdone as to be clichés, and unless the twist is 'earned', it will come across as contrived, resulting in a story with what I see as an eel-like shape with a ribbon for a tail. The 'twist' endings had their belle epoque during Edgar Allan Poe's time, and perhaps a bit beyond, but since Chekhov and Carver, the postmodern consciousness can be deeply suspicious of these 'twist' endings where characters conveniently die or come back from the dead, or *Deus Ex Machina* saves the day, or lots of red herrings were thrown in the story to deceive and it turns out that one throwaway fact was the key to unlock the whole story. They can feel like 'cheap gimmicks' or even 'egoism' where the author holds all the cards and only chooses to reveal them at the very end.

On the other hand, surprising or 'remarkable' endings, *when organically grown*, can often bring great aesthetic pleasure and satisfaction. But how is it different from a 'twist' ending?

Alice Munro is a progenitor of the 'surprise' ending. In her story, *Floating Bridge*, the elephant in the room is Jinny's cancer. This is a story about how Jinny handles the news, in the immediate aftermath, that her tumor has shrunk significantly. There's nothing conventional about the plot twists Munro chooses. Rather than opening with Jinny telling her husband Neal the surprising good news, which is how I might have opened, Munro brings in her first surprise — a young volunteer named Helen who's hired to help Jinny in her illness, and who's forgotten to bring along a pair of shoes. We see Neal driving to pick up the shoes from Helen's sister in a state of 'invaded' bliss. Helen's sister does not have them. Another surprise here when we see Neal wheedling and teasing until Helen agrees to show them the way to the Bergsons, her foster home, to retrieve her shoes. On arrival, the Bergsons insist they come in for leftover chilli, but by this time, Jinny just wants to be alone. She is nauseous and tired, and she has not yet told Neal the good news.

We see Neal's state of bliss evaporate, replaced with irritation at Jinny's rebuff of the Bergsons' country hospitality. We realize he is not available for Jinny. While Neal goes inside, Jinny heads into a cornfield with the singular thought of lying down and getting some rest and shade from the unremitting sun. While there, she begins to stew about a silly psychological game she'd played with a group of people and their candid opinions about her. Really, she is angry at Neal for misunderstanding her. Jinny experiences a little epiphany. 'When you died, these wrong opinions were all there was left.' Lo and behold, lost in thought, Jinny gets lost in the cornfield and emerges only by following the direction of Matt Bergson's voice, come to offer her chilli again. While Matt Bergson begins to tell her a ribald, off-color joke, Jinny begins to process the news the doctor has given her. Out loud, she says, 'it's too much', offending Matt, who says he will take up no more of her time.

Characteristic of the Munro capacity to surprise, Jinny then pees on the ground of the Bergson's yard, not just symbolic of her feelings towards their in-your-face hospitality, but also, heart-breakingly, because she's taken to wearing long skirts and no knickers, given her lack of bowel control. It's just so much easier to pee wherever and whenever you need to.

The Bergsons' son, a young waiter, arrives home. He has an uncanny knack for telling time without a watch, and gallantly, he seems to sense Jinny's mental muddle and offers to drive her home. In a story full of one surprising twist after another, he is perhaps the most surprising of all—this least likely of knights errant, this serendipitous time-keeper. He takes her to a floating bridge where he kisses her and is elated at kissing a married woman for the first time. For Jinny too, this is a first, and she feels a kind of tender hilarity for the new life she'd been given.

Rendering surprise upon surprise in a story can feel random, off-the-wall. In *Floating Bridge*, it comes close to a sort of genius. I love how this story surprises me on every page. I'm mystified by the kiss. I love the 'tender hilarity', not a response I expected. Munro could have written a very straightforward story. That she chose to take unpredictable tacks left and right compelled us to understand Jinny's inability to take in her good news. Everything happening to her afterwards mirrors the surprise she's been handed, including the ultimate surprise at the end—the border-line inappropriate kiss. The floating bridge she stands on with the young man becomes a metaphor for that temporary ineffable state she's in. Munro used the element of 'surprise' not just to keep freshening our expectations, but also because it's deeply interior to this character's response to her situation. It was an organic choice.

MIRROR / CIRCULAR ENDINGS

What about the mirror ending, where the ending returns full circle to the image or scene or metaphor of the beginning?

I tend to use this sparingly, not because life doesn't come full circle, but because it rarely does. It's far more rewarding for me to read a story where the main character arrives at a different place than where she started, like Jinny above. If there's any circularity that one can pinpoint, it's that the ending of one story is often the beginning of another. Here are the endings of three rather famous short stories. Every one of them could have been the beginning sentence of another.

> *'I feel fine,' she said. 'There's nothing wrong with me. I feel fine.'*
> Ernest Hemingway — 'Hills Like White Elephants'

> *The tide of darkness seemed to sweep him back to her, postponing from moment to moment his entry into the world of guilt and sorrow.*
> Flannery O'Connor — 'Everything that Rises Must Converge'

> *And I am sitting at my mother's place at the mah jong table, on the East, where things begin.*
> Amy Tan — 'Joy Luck Club'

And the beginning sentences of some seem to work just as well for endings.

> *Stella, cold, cold, the coldness of hell.*
>   Cynthia Ozick — 'The Shawl'

> *To put us at our ease, to quiet our hearts as she lay dying, our dear friend Selena said, Life, after all, has not been an unrelieved horror —you know, I did have many wonderful years with her.*
>   Grace Paley — 'Friends'

> *My husband eats with a good appetite. But I don't think he's really hungry. He chews, arms on the table, and stares at something across the room. He looks at me and looks away. He wipes his mouth on the napkin. He shrugs, and goes on eating.*
>   Raymond Carver — 'So Much Water So Close to Home'

I can't help but think of my mother-in-law, how true it was that her story had ended, but ours—the story of how we remember her—has just begun.

RESONANT ENDINGS

While not every ending should contain an epiphany, I believe it has to be resonant. Crafting a resonant ending is, dare I say it, a little bit of witchcraft. Incredibly hard to pull off without keeping the shape, the entirety, of your story in mind. *Cheap* resonance, on the other hand, is a dime a dozen—cheap, plasticky, usually those dime-store bromides that trip off a main character's tongue in the manner of an epiphany, but true resonance is a skilful blend of metaphor, scene, emotions, objects, thoughts and imagery. Everything in the story brings you to this point where the 'tail' of your ending begins.

A resonant ending makes you want to do what Salman Rushdie says in BASS 2008, 'get up and clap'. Nicole Krauss' story from this collection, *At The Desk of Daniel Varsky*, achieves this with an effortlessness bordering on magic. Our protagonist—a poetess—has broken up with R, and finds herself furnitureless, after R's had been removed. A friend tells her about a Chilean poet, Daniel Varsky, who's willing to loan her some of his furniture, as he's about to head back to Chile. Daniel is a poet hungering for experience and burning with the fires of socialism for the future of his native country. Among the pieces of furniture is a clunky desk with lots of drawers that Varsky tells her was once used by Lorca. They meet only once, during which they talk for seven to eight hours about poetry and everything else that moves them. Varsky reads her one of his poems which strikes her as being about a girl who'd broken his heart, but the poem has the effect of reminding her of R and produces a tripartite response of wanting to cry and laugh and choke.

Varsky tells her he's entrusting her with the furniture, and plans to reclaim them when he returns to New York. 'Suddenly,' our narrator says, 'I felt awash in gratitude to their owner, as if he were handing down to me not just some wood and upholstery but the chance at a new life, leaving it up to me to rise to the occasion.'

They kiss, which is anticlimactic, but later, this get-together is imbued with a sad and fathoms-deep nostalgia for our narrator. Many years later, she hears that Daniel Varsky has been taken in the middle of the night by Manuel Contreras's secret police. He is never seen again. Our poetess continues to use Daniel Varsky's desk for the next thirty years, but she stops writing poetry.

> . . . I felt trapped in the poems I tried to write, which is like saying one feels trapped in the universe, or trapped by the inevitability of death, but the truth of why I stopped writing poetry is not any of these, not nearly, not exactly. The truth is that if I could explain why I stopped writing poetry then I might write it again. What I am saying is that Daniel Varsky's desk, which became my desk, . . . reminds me of these things. I've always considered myself only a temporary guardian and had assumed a day would come, after which, albeit with mixed feelings, I would be relieved of my responsibility, the responsibility of living with and watching over the furniture of my friend, the dead poet Daniel Varsky . . .

As if the narrator is telling us: that night so long ago, Daniel Varsky had a foreshadowing that he might possibly not return and so, to our protagonist he entrusts his soul to keep, in the form of a desk and other furniture.

And finally, here's how Nicole Krauss ends this story, knocking resonance out of the ballpark, bringing the story home. There is one drawer located just above her right knee that has remained locked these thirty-odd years. She's never found the key.

> For some reason I always assumed that the drawer contained letters from the girl in the poem Daniel Varsky once read to me, or if not her, then someone like her. But as I write this it occurs to me that I don't know where I ever got that idea. In fact, I have no memory of whether

the desk arrived to me with the drawer locked. It's possible that I unknowingly pushed in the cylindrical lock years ago, and that whatever is in there belongs to me.

The bits stuffed in a drawer are likely all the flotsam from our past life we don't care to examine, the regrets and lost opportunities of great love, great poetry, great understanding and resplendent clarity, that we let run through our fingers because we, unlike Daniel Varsky, may not believe in guardian angels—in itself a kind of ideology—and we, unlike him, don't have someone to entrust it to. Our narrator doesn't say all this—it's the broken lines—the underbelly of the 'fish', and if our writer has done her work, our protagonist doesn't have to.

How do you leave your stories? Can you entrust it to your character to let you know when it's time to go?

 ## REFERENCE WORKS AND FAVOURITE STORIES

Baxter, Charles. *Burning Down The House: Essays on Fiction.* (Graywolf Press, 1997)

Carver, Raymond. 'So Much Water So Close to Home.' *What We Talk About When We Talk About Love: Stories* (Vintage Book Contemporaries, 1989)

Chekhov, Anton. 'Gusev.' *Forty Stories* (Vintage Classics, 1991)

———, 'The Lady with the Lap Dog', ibid.

Dark, Alice Elliott. 'In The Gloaming.' *The Best American Short Stories of the Century.* Ed. John Updike. Co-ed. Katrina Kennison. (Houghton Mifflin, 1999)

Hemingway, Ernest. 'Hills Like White Elephants.' *The Oxford Book of Short Stories*. Ed. V.S. Pritchett. (Oxford University Press, 1981)

Joyce, James. 'Araby.' *Great Short Stories of the Masters*. (First Cooper Square Press edition, 2002)

Krauss, Nicole. 'At the Desk of Daniel Varsky.' *The Best American Short Stories 2008*. Ed. Salman Rushdie. Series Ed. Heidi Pitlor (Houghton Mifflin Harcourt Publishing, 2008)

Moore, Lorrie. 'Which Is More Than You Can Say About Some People.' *Birds of America*. (Faber and Faber Limited, 1998)

———. 'Community Life.' *Birds of America*, ibid.

———. 'People Like That Are The Only People Here.' *Birds of America*, ibid.

———. 'You're Ugly, Too.' *The Best American Short Stories of the Century*. Ed. John Updike. Co-ed. Katrina Kennison. (Houghton Mifflin, 1999)

Munro, Alice. 'Floating Bridge.' *Hateship, Friendship, Courtship, Loveship, Marriage*. (Chatto & Windus, 2001)

O'Connor, Flannery. 'Everything That Rises Must Converge.' *The Complete Stories*. (Faber and Faber, 2000)

Ofutt, Chris. 'Getting It Straight'. Sfwp.org, a literary journal (Santa Fe Writing Project). http://sfwp.org/archives/22

Ozick, Cynthia. 'The Shawl.' *The Best American Short Stories of the Century*. Ed. John Updike. Co-ed. Katrina Kennison. (Houghton Mifflin, 1999)

Paley, Grace. 'Friends'. *The Collected Stories*. (Virago Press, 1999)

Tan, Amy. 'Joy Luck Club.' *The Granta Book of the American Short Story*. Ed. Richard Ford. (Granta Books, 1998)

IDEAS FOR FURTHER EXPLORATION

ONE

Take any Alice Munro story that you haven't read or have forgotten much of how the story went, and read the beginning. From there, weave your own story. Afterwards compare and analyze each of your plot twist with the original. Do her plot twists surprise you or are there similarities?

TWO

Swap stories with a writing friend. Take her ending sentence and begin your own story from that point.

PAUL MAGRS

THOUGHTS ABOUT WRITING FICTION, AT THE END OF TERM

Every year — for as long as I can remember — I have run fiction workshops. Usually I'm in the middle of writing fiction of my own while I'm teaching other people. It keeps me on my toes. I learn so much from the students, every year. By the end of a course your head ends up swirling with all these thoughts and ideas about stories and how to write them. All the answers are there, somewhere . . . in amongst all your notes about stories written by eighteen other people . . . if you could just assemble the notes into some order . . . that's the thing.

Here are some thoughts I had at the end of a recent term of writing workshops. Think of them as notes down the margins of double-spaced pages of prose. Here we go — in no particular order:

- Beware of too much going on in one sentence.
- When you break a scene and leave a very dramatic, white

pause between sections, be consistent in what the gap represents. Is it a shift in time, place or point of view?

- Is 'engulfed' too fancy a verb? Verbs are so important to get right. They have to be muscular. They keep the prose and the story going, and the tension up . . . and that's (one of the things) keeping the reader reading.

- What?? What does this mean? Is it wilfully obscure and knotty? Are we supposed to be puzzled by this? There's an art to being mystifying; to learning to intrigue your reader. It's about stringing them along—but also about learning how not to piss them off. Don't lose them.

- Cluttered sentences. Nasty show-off sentences. Trying to sound too writerly. By 'writerly' I mean someone's idea of what a piece of fiction should sound like, ie, someone's rubbishy, middlebrow idea. Don't try to sound like someone else. Especially someone rubbishy and middlebrow.

- Keep your action sequences simple. Tell them clearly. We have to picture this stuff. We have to be able to see it.

- Too many characters coming in at once? You'll make the reader want to scream. Assume that readers are lazy. If they get too much info all at once, they'll stop trying. Let each character register, and make their impact. Underline and underscore their presences with physical, concrete detail, with tics and traits. Repeat them just enough on each reappearance.

- Don't—as writer—assume that the reader knows about and can see the characters as well as you can. Don't assume we know how old they are, for example, or what the relationships between them are. You have to smuggle and shoehorn that kind of information in, very subtly, very carefully. Don't deluge us with info.

- Don't explain too much.

- Why's your writing getting overly formal and ornate? Why's it become show-offy? Usually it's because you've run out of story.

- If things have gone a bit rococo, ask yourself: Who is narrating this story? Whose voice is this? From what point in time? Does this voice betray an attitude towards the characters and their milieu? Should it?

- Adverbs can be great. Mostly, they're shit. Mostly, they're used shitly. They soften the impact of a verb. They betray hesitations on the writer's part. Especially when they are words like 'fairly', 'actually', 'seemingly.' Just think about the redundancies in current clichés of speech; those dreadful adverbial doings: 'literally,' 'basically', 'at the end of the day . . .' These are phrases that mean nothing. They're good in dialogue, though.

- People talk such shit. Let's hear it.

- Time has to move. Begin with events and keep them going. This sounds obvious, but it doesn't always occur to people. They think they can hold back time—and explain everything to us at great length—like Rod Serling used to in *The Twilight Zone*.

- Time has to move. Keep it moving and fold all the info we need into the mix—but don't stop to explain too much. Don't get mired down.

- Be aware of how much it's possible for a reader to remember. Discover more about how your own memory works when it comes to reading. Ask other people how their memories work. Can they reconstruct the four dimensions of a story in their heads? Do they reconstruct it backwards or forward, or from a point in the middle? Do they remember characters or plot beats? Ideas or sensations?

- Don't neglect to include crucial plot beats. The reader will know if you've left out an important step in the unfolding of the plot. These are what Roland Barthes used to call 'cardinal functions' — ie, important stuff happening, that will lead to other, important stuff. Different to 'indicial functions' — which is all the atmosphere and detail and richness. Make them work together. You need both: pushing forward, as well as depth and richness. They're in constant tension, but don't neglect either. One impulse wants to push onwards; the other wants to dwell in the moment. A constantly shifting balance is necessary.

- Learn how to feed necessary exposition to your reader. If it's unsubtle the reader will feel preached at. They'll realise this is 'important' plot beat stuff they'll need to remember, and they'll probably skip it. Avoid having a character feed us exposition by letting them dwell on recent events inside their heads. This holds up the action. It freezes time. You've got to think: can this exposition possibly be done in dialogue, in real time? And then you can let your reader eavesdrop. The reader feels flattered by that, rather than patronised. If they earwig on a conversation filled with clues, they feel that they're being given something meaty to work out. They don't want to be given all the answers on a plate. Also, the reader likes the clandestine feeling of eavesdropping. There's a frisson of pleasure to that.

- Mention delicious smells. Gorgeous colours. Music. Art. Food. Sexy goings-on at any opportunity. Epiphanies of all kinds. Don't forget to appeal to all our senses. Make the bodily and the intellectual and the emotional try to meet up in sensations we can imagine. Seduce the reader with these moments.

- Give the reader pleasure whenever you can . . .
- Writers starting out always get meta-discursive at every opportunity. Every single writer seems to do this! They adopt a godlike narrator's voice that starts to question its authority, that starts to play literary games with the reader, and clever-clever tricks on the reader. Or the protagonist is a writer who tells us all about stories and the nature of truth and illusion. *Aaaaaggggghhhhh!* This is your first story! Nothing's happening! Get on with it! Stop playing with narrative form and ideas of intentionality and trying to shift bleeding paradigms! You got into this stuff in the first place because you liked making up stories! What's your problem? Why have you stopped?
- How come it's only paragraph one and you're already up your own arse?
- All this stuff is a symptom of the writer dealing with their own assumed authority. These are metaphors and strategies to delay the writing process; the actual business of making things up; the embarrassing business of having characters actually do things and saying 'he said, she said'. It's about avoiding the task in hand. Do I dare invent?? JUST DO IT!
- If you're doing some kind of literary pastiche (Oh, Jesus — at UEA it was always Nabokov, Rushdie, Pynchon, Eco, Amis) you REALLY have to know what it is you're meant to be pastiching. If you're going to play all the literary games and flag up the literariness and all that jazz — if you're going to mess about with the textiness of the text — its writtenness — then you really have got to get it right.

(There's nothing worse than a half-cocked go at flagging up your materiality.)

- Usually, in your first draft—your first splurge of writing—there is a fabulous detail or image or event or idea on about page two, or three. Most often, two thirds of the way down page two. This is where the whole thing should start. This is when you warmed up. Be brutal. Cut out everything up until that point. Start there, at the good bit. That's your hook.

- Don't let it get messy. Correct small typos all the time. Vigilance. Use that time as thinking time, when you're still inside the text, tinkering about. It's like musicians, tuning up between songs, changing snapped and fraying strings.

- You can learn an awful lot about stories-within-stories, framing devices, flashbacks and points of view from old movies. All the tools are there. Movies are good for writers because they are stripped down: you can hold the whole shape of one in your head. Like a short story, perhaps. Certainly more easily, sometimes, than you can a novel. Movies keep time moving and demonstrate how time works because all movies are, necessarily, all about time.

- Make us laugh. What would be the point of a piece of writing without jokes?

- Fancy syntax turns to crap in some people's mouths. Calm it down.

- Archaic language. 'Akin,' 'Beholden.' What?? I blame the Bible. Listen to how people speak now. 'At the end of the day, like, it's literally the time you're, like, living in, yeah?'

- Learn to have a lighter touch. In a dramatic scene, give us the words, events and gestures. If necessary, let your character reflect on it later. While the scene's happening, let the reader do the reacting. Don't tell the reader what to think or feel. Don't muffle the impact of a scene by having everyone thinking all the time. When every single response and reaction is nailed down and spelled out, all the fun goes out of things. It stops being dramatic and edgy. Leave some gaps. Fiction needs to have everyday chaos in it. Fiction needs mystery in it. It needs gaps in it, for us to mull over . . .

- First person narrators. Everyone loves writing these — because they think they're easy to do. They aren't.

- How does a first person narrator manage to give a strong enough sense of themselves to the reader? Without it seeming like they're telling you too much and banging on?

- We have to see them in action; living through time. We have to see them perform live, as it were. Then we can make up our own minds. We're very close to them, when they speak to us in their own voices. Are we close to someone we like, or someone we despise?

- A first person narrator can (or thinks that they can) stack the deck, in terms of what the reader finds out. They think they can have it all their own way. For the reader, it's like having a very bossy friend, or someone standing extremely close to you — chatting on and on and on. They try to dominate your view of this world.

- The skilled writer will make the first person narrator say things they don't mean to. They will slip, and give themselves away. The reader will glimpse their world — and unspoken truths about it — over their shoulder . . .

- J.D. Salinger 'For Esme, with Love and Squalor'; F. Scott Fitzgerald 'The Great Gatsby'; Christopher Isherwood 'Goodbye to Berlin'. By Spring 1990, when I was twenty, I had read these three again and again. I've read thousands of books since, but I don't think I've learned nearly as much from anything since reading those three at that stage in my dealing with writing.

- Remember: Clever is good. Clever-clever is shit. Clever-clever-clever is good again.
- I don't know why.

(This essay appeared in a slightly different form in *Transmission* magazine)

 ## FAVOURITE SHORT STORIES

'Lamb to the Slaughter' by Roald Dahl can be found online at Classic Shorts: www.classicshorts.com

'Mad About The Boy' by Georgina Hammick from *The Best of Fiction Magazine*, ed. Cooke & Bunster, J.M. Dent 1986

'In Dreams Begin Responsibilities' by Delmore Schwartz , from the collection of the same title (New Directions Publishing Corporation 1978)

'Present for a Good Girl' by Nadine Gordimer, from *Harrap's Modern English—Short Stories of Our Time* Ed Barnes (Nelson Thornes 1999)

'Life of Ma Parker' by Katherine Mansfield can be found online at www.readbookonline.net

VANESSA GEBBIE

LEAVING THE DOOR AJAR: ON SHORT STORY OPENINGS . . .

Imagine you are walking down a corridor. It is lined with doors, all different colours. Some are closed, the majority are ajar. Just a chink. You can only go into one room, and you want it to be an interesting one, one in which you will spend a memorable hour or so. From what you can see or hear through some of the doors, or the gaps, something is happening in every room. You catch a glimpse of people, some talking, some quiet. A glimpse of their lives—different places, even different worlds. You hear enticing sounds. Music, conversation or even something unidentifiable. Maybe a door or two is wider open. You hear blaring music, see flashing lights, people rushing hither and thither; chaotic. Maybe in another room it is pale, bland, silent, and one depressed looking character is sitting on the floor doing very little. You can only touch one door.

To make it harder, the doors are heavy. To get into the room of your choice, you have to push.

And what exactly has this to do with writing short stories, and especially opening them? This. Your reader is in that corridor. The corridor is a magazine, a journal, a slush pile, an anthology, a hundred entries for a competition. You want them to pick *your* room.

That's about where the analogy wears thin. When you are writing, if you worry too much about 'other people', markets, the battle for publication, your work may not come easily. It is easy to lean on other published writers' styles, because they've 'made it' whatever that means. But who on earth wants to write like anyone else? You want to write like *you* and still be read.

Maybe there is another way to look at the door left ajar. Think of a seduction scene. Simplistically, 'A' wants 'B' — and is very aware of all the ploys and games he could employ to achieve the objective. If he is too obvious and strips off shouting 'Hey, how's about bed, darlin'?' 'B' might well run a mile. That's the wide open door, if you like. The big bang opener. Or even the exhibitionist who makes the story all about himself and his writing — not about the story.

But if 'A' is too obtuse and says or does nothing much, before long target 'B' will be smooching with someone else. Being simplistic again, that's the opening that diddles about commenting on the weather. Or introduces a bland character who doesn't seem to do much of interest until page four, if the reader gets that far, and the result is that we lose interest fast.

But — sticking with the seduction analogy — if 'A' uses the right body language, says the right things, and makes 'B' interested enough to stay around to find out more — the door is left slightly open. 'B' stays and talks, becomes more and more interested, wants to know more about 'A'. And before 'B' knows it, 'B' is hooked.

I'd argue that the opener to a successful short story has to raise a question fairly fast in the reader's mind. And do it in such a way that the reader is intrigued enough to read on to the next sentence, the next paragraph. Each step is an investment that takes them further and further into the 'room' of the story. They are pushing open the door.

Think of the questions the reader might ask were he/she to be vocalising the slide into the story.

'Who am I spending the next half hour with?' (Character—you need to introduce the main character, if not a minor character or two. How? Do you describe them, let them speak for the reader to 'hear' them? Maybe the characters should do something quickly, to let the reader see them in action?)

'Why should I want to spend the next half hour with *this* character, and not turn to another story/go and make tea/ phone a friend/ go for a run/watch a film/go to sleep?' (You have to make your reader *feel* something. A twitch of caring about the situation enough to want to read on. Some people will say 'you need to introduce a 'hook' here.' Raise a question about the character that needs answering. Whatever—the reader must feel involved enough to care, at this point.)

'Where am I?' (Setting. You need to give a sense of place. That may be thanks to description. It may be thanks to voice. Language. The senses.)

'What sort of story is this?' (All part of setting out the contract with the reader—what is the emotional temperature of this story? Is this is a comedy, a thoughtful piece, a crime story, a tragedy . . . ? You need to give some thought to the emotional tone of the piece.)

'Will the prose itself be any good?' (Your wobbling reader needs to begin to feel confident. That investing his time in your work will be worth it. That you will deliver a story well enough for him to forget he is reading . . .)

I think the best way to feel what a good opener is, is to look at a few.

The very first thing your reader meets, the first chance you have to intrigue them, the first poser of questions, is your title. Go now, if you can, and pick up a few short story anthologies. Maybe ones you don't know well yet. (It's a fairly safe bet that if you are reading this, you will have a few around.) Take a look at the contents page. And select one or two titles that begin to lead you somewhere, make you want to turn to that story.

I wonder if you have picked one word titles, like these from an anthology or two I have just looked at: 'Swimming', 'Rash', 'Birth', 'History'—or whether you have chosen titles that seem to open up ideas, raise a smile, raise a question—again, from a pile of anthologies on the floor next to me: 'Beethoven was One-Sixteenth Black', 'After Cowboy Chicken Came to Town', 'How to Murder Your Mother', 'The Angel in the Car Park', 'The Incredible Exploding Victor'. I know which stories I would turn to first, and it isn't the one-word lot above, great as those stories may well be, in the end.

Your title is vitally important. Treat it with care. If you are at a loss, decide what the story is really 'about' (and I do not mean subject matter, I mean theme . . .) and find a phrase from the story that encapsulates your theme. Find an appropriate quote from a poem, maybe from Shakespeare. Try taking a few images from the story and making them into a title. I did this once and came up with 'Yellow Diggers, Dead Crows, Gifts'. It's a bit cumbersome, but it worked for the story. It did OK 'out there', then I changed the title to 'Dodie's Gift', and it did well again. A title that incorporates the name of the main character can work wonders — after all, the reader has been introduced very fast.

Then those first few lines have got to work seriously hard for the story. Think of what the reader needs to feel. Intrigue, first. Fascination for something in those lines. Character perhaps. The reader has to feel secure in his growing suspicion that this character will be worth investing the next half hour or more. Or there needs to be something unusual about the setting, something worth investigating.

How do you make your character intriguing from the start? Look at this opener, from 'The Keeper of the Virgins', by Hanan Al-Shaykh, and consider these lines in the light of the title of the story:

> One of the women wondered aloud if he was a dwarf in every way. The other women sitting at the intersection burst out laughing.

And this, from 'The First and Final Continent', by Jhumpa Lahiri:

> I left India in 1964 with a certificate in commerce and the equivalent, in those days, of ten dollars to my name.

And, from one of my favourite stories, 'The Raft', by Peter Orner:

> My grandfather, who lost his short-term memory sometime during the first Eisenhower administration, calls me into his study because he wants to tell me the story he has never told anybody before, again.

Look what these lines do. How very hard they are working, for all their simplicity.

How do you make a setting intriguing? Look at this opener from 'North Cold' by Tania Hershman:

> There is a small town in the north that is cold all year round. The people living there have come to accept it as they accept that the sun sets and the sun rises. Cold is the natural order of things. No-one talks about the weather, except visitors, who do not stay for longer than they must. The people of this town have thicker skin than those living elsewhere; here, people live further inside themselves.

Here, the setting segues neatly into character. It is as important as the people in this story, and the whole opener sets up a sense of fable.

The best openers, for this reader, are stories where, thanks to some alchemy between writing, title, character and setting, I am transported immediately into a fictive dream, sinking into the world created for me by the writer. Look at this by Zimbabwean writer Petina Gappah, the opening to the title story from her collection *An Elegy for Easterly*:

> It was the children who first noticed that there was something different about the woman they called Martha Mupengo. They followed her, as they often did, past the houses at Easterly Farm, houses of pole and mud, of thick black plastic sheeting for walls and clear plastic for windows, houses that erupted without City permission . . .

How you choreograph those first few paragraphs, how well you balance the craft elements, will dictate how successfully your reader is taken up in your world. You have one chance to entice the reader to come along with you, and it is all a question of balance.

Easy as they may seem, it is a certainty that those short story openings above did not just happen, in the majority of cases. What appear to be effortless, easy drifting sentences were probably worked at, agonised over, rewritten many many times.

I wonder how much the writers consciously used a mental checklist when they wrote their first drafts . . . 'must show interesting character, setting, ah, and title. Secondary characters. A bit of dialogue to dramatise. Have I got enough intrigue here?' I doubt it. I know that if I *try* to plot, *try* to write a coherent story, it is like walking thigh deep in molasses and the story is weighed down by all that gunk.

In case it is useful, here is how I started one story. And how it took me a couple of years to do that opening. I pick this one because the stretched-out process allows me to look back and see it stage by stage. The story is called 'Words from a Glass Bubble'.

A few years back I had an idea for a character. A statuette of the Virgin Mary who talks to a woman. 'Hey! That's nice,' I thought. 'I like that.' I was fond of the Don Camillo stories by Giovanni Guareschi as a schoolgirl, and inspiration came through decades later.

I duly started the opening paragraph, describing the statuette. Lovely appropriate language (hopefully . . .), pensive and weighty, flowing lines for the robes, a little face looking out at the world, peaceful and thoughtful . . . and when I came to the female character, nothing. A shadow pottering about.

The story died very quickly.

Now. I could have written a 'something', obviously. I could have scribbled a yarn. But I was told years back that writers can 'grab at' stories far too quickly, without letting them simmer in the subconscious. 'Stories,' so says Dorothea Brande, 'are formed in the unconscious mind, which must flow freely and richly, bringing together all the 'treasures of memory, all the emotions, scenes, incidents, intimations of character and relationship' which are stored away beyond our awareness. It is a question of trusting your own creative processes. They *will* deliver.'

So, that story only died for the moment. Stories have a life of their own. They come and go as they please, if you let them. Almost a year later, I was reminded of this unwritten story when I saw a graveyard in Ireland, the graves littered with plastic statuettes encased in glass bubbles. I started the story again, describing a woman walking through a graveyard, and coming across a child's grave complete with statuette in said bubble.

Please notice the words 'I' and 'describing' there? I was in control, again, consciously looking for nice words. Playing at being a writer. (Have you met that one? It goes like this . . . 'I am a writer. I must write well, and convince my reader that I am special at what I do.') And like all games, the end came along fairly quickly. The story died. Again. But I had something new. The story was 'about' a child in some way. And loss. Not surprising; they are well-explored subjects for this writer.

I tried to write that opening so many times. And I failed so many times. Probably because I was *trying* to write it. In the end, almost at the point of giving up, I remember thinking 'what's actually *happening* here?' sitting down to remind myself of the basics—and the opening wrote itself in a few minutes. Brande would say my subconscious had done its work and was letting the story go:

The Virgin Mary spoke to Eva Duffy from a glass bubble in a niche halfway up the stairs. Eva, the post woman, heard the words in her stomach more than in her ears, and she called her the VM. The VM didn't seem to mind. She was plastic, six inches high, hand painted, and appeared to be growing out of a mass of very green foliage, more suited to a fish tank. She held a naked Infant Jesus who stretched his arms out to Eva and mouthed every so often, 'Carry?'

The VM's words were unfailingly meaningful, but often ungrammatical . . .

As I wrote that (it took as long as it just took to retype it) I had *no conscious idea* that Eva called the statuette anything. I had *no idea* that the infant spoke, or that he would act like a real toddler. I had *no idea* that the statuette spoke anything but perfectly.

Eva Duffy was writing her story. I was just typing for her. As I typed, the statuette came to life. Eva came to life. And a husband wandered into the shot. Huh? I hadn't even thought of a husband figure:

'It will be the porcelain and silver effigies that speak properly,' Eva said. And anyway, this VM had to speak out of the corner of her mouth where her pink lipstick had smudged.

She also appeared to have a wall eye. That would be the sloppy painting in the VM factory, according to Connor, Eva's bricklayer husband, who never stopped on the stairs to find out if she spoke to him too. 'No one's perfect,' Eva said.

Connor had a port wine stain on his left cheek in the shape of Cyprus with a few undiscovered islands under his ear.

Rewind. I tried too hard time and time again to write a story about a statuette and a woman. I should have trusted my own processes enough to know that I need my characters first, and they won't form without a gestation period. Thank you Dorothea Brande, for teaching me that I need to wait.

If you go back and look at those short paragraphs, written as I said in a few minutes—but the *right* few minutes, what have you got?

Tone. This is gentle, with a wry humour. It is not going to be uproariously funny, but it will have a lightness about it.

Character. Three characters introduced. Questions posed. Gentle intrigue.

Setting: A niche at the turn of the stairs. Plastic trimmings. A cheap little statuette. A post woman and her bricklayer husband. It's all there, isn't it? Did I need any more?

The weather? I have no idea, because it is not relevant!

The most important thing for me, looking back, is how I *felt* when writing this. I was excited. I didn't know where I was going. I didn't know what any of my three characters would say or do next. They were making me laugh. I was feeling sad, as well. I knew there would be something about the loss of a child . . . and isn't the image of the Virgin Mary also to do with the loss of a son, whether one is a believer in the strictest sense or not? Suddenly, I understood that the story was on its way. It had taken over.

It was time, and waiting for character to form that had done that. In asking the simple question 'What's happening here?' I had unlocked the characters. Because things don't just happen in a vacuum. They happen TO people.

So, if I can lend you a tip that I find works over and over and over again . . . it is to suggest you ask yourself that same question.

What is happening? The story will start itself *in media res*, in the middle of the action, and you'll be well on the way down the road.

I hope I've shown that I didn't just set an idea loose to come up with a great opening paragraph or two. I spent a long time learning my craft. And I am still learning At least, I hope so! That's fundamental.

And it is also why this essay comes at the end of the book, after all the craft talk, all the insights into the *how and why* of all the generous writers in this book. Because without learning, chances are that newer writers may write a yarn or two — but may not write as well as they are able.

I spent years, not just practising writing short stories myself, but reading craft articles, reading good short fiction, measuring what I was doing against the best. And most importantly, critiquing regularly. Analysing the work of not only my peers but also writers who were far more experienced than I am. Taking their stories to pieces, offering considered and honest feedback illustrated with text examples. Analysing published work too.

So, when I came to the story above, and when I had let it stew for as long as it needed to, out it came aided and abetted by a lot of hard work and a good understanding of craft.

You will hear some writers saying 'the story wrote itself', as if this writing of fiction, short or long, is easy. They may ask you to believe they woke up one morning able to write prize-winning fiction. I'm sure that must have happened to one or two, but generally, that is not how it works, believe me! It takes graft.

I make no apologies for requoting Faulkner from the introduction:

Let the writer take up surgery or bricklaying if he is interested in technique. There is no mechanical way to get the writing done, no shortcut. The young writer would be a fool to follow a theory. Teach yourself by your own mistakes; people learn only by error.

But when it comes right, it is the best feeling in the world.

 # REFERENCE BOOKS

'The Keeper Of The Virgins' by Hanan Al Shaikh is from *The Art of the Story, an International Anthology of Short Stories* edited by Daniel Halpern. (Penguin USA, 2000)

'The First and Final Continent' by Jhumpa Lahiri is from her collection *The Interpreter of Maladies*. (Mariner Books, 1999)

'The Raft' by Peter Orner is from *The Best American Short Stories of 2001* edited by Barbara Kingsolver. (Houghton Mifflin, 2001)

'North Cold' by Tania Hershman is from her collection *The White Road and other Stories* (Salt, 2008)

'An Elegy for Easterly' by Petina Gappah is from her collection *An Elegy for Easterly* (Faber and Faber, 2009)

'Words from a Glass Bubble' is from my own collection, *Words from a Glass Bubble* (Salt, 2008).

Dorothea Brande's words are from *Becoming a Writer* by Dorothea Brande (Jeremy P. Tarcher, 1981).

FAVOURITE SHORT STORIES

'The Moon Above his Head' by Yann Martel in *Freedom*, the Amnesty International Anthology (Mainstream, 2009)

'Light is Like Water' by Gabriel Garcia Marquez, from *Strange Pilgrims* (Penguin, 1994)

'The Raft' by Peter Orner is online at Atlantic Online here: www.theatlantic.com

'A Small Good Thing' by Raymond Carver (*Best American Short Stories of the Century*, Ed: John Updike. Houghton Mifflin, 2000)

'Midnight at The Hotel California' by Petina Gappah, from *Elegy for Easterly* (Faber and Faber, 2009)

'The Swimmer' by John Cheever from *Collected Stories* (Vintage, 1900)

'The Twenty-Seventh Man' by Nathan Englander, from *For the Relief of Unbearable Urges* (Vintage, 2000)

'Ballistics' by Alex Keegan, from *Ballistics* (Salt, 2008)

 IDEAS FOR FURTHER EXPLORATION

ONE

Take the opening to a published story and re-write the opening as many times as you like. Try looking at the opening from the point of view of another character in the story. If it is written in third person, rewrite it in first person. And vice versa. Try second person as well. Then use the same events/setting/details . . . and change the style of the writing. If it is chatty and open, make it more formal. If it is distanced, make it more intimate. Try out all sorts of permutations.

What was it that made the actual opening work so well? Chances are that the writer tried out a lot of the same things as you just did.

Repeat this with one of your own stories. Try things out. Look at the story from all directions. Surprise yourself . . .

TWO

Using one of the openers quoted in the essay above, carry on and write your own story. Use this in a group — its great fun seeing where our different journeys go, what different stories can grow from the same seeds. The best results come if you don't know the actual story. Compare your stories and the original. Did they share anything?

VANESSA GEBBIE

SHORT STORY COMPETITIONS: HARD WORK, PERSISTENCE, LUCK AND A BOWL OF FRUIT

We send off our manuscripts to competitions, and whisper 'Good luck' either as we hit the submit button, or the envelope falls into the post box. We know our stories are going to find their way into a pile of anonymous entries, and depending on the competition, that pile might be thousands strong. But is luck anything to do with your story being picked for long listing, short listing or final placing?

The answer to that is yes, a little bit, and I will explain why. But also, it is possible to increase your chances of a story catching the eye of the reader, and I'll also say something about that. And about persistence, because placing at Bridport and a couple of times at Fish, coming first in a few others- has not happened overnight. It has taken a few years of slog and stubbornness.

I have chatted at length to the final judge and to the readers for both the Bridport Prize, and the Fish Short Story Prize, finding out what they look for. And it might surprise you. They did not talk about being concerned with a deliberate search for technical perfection, sparkling prose, all the elements of fiction honed and polished to produce a virtuoso piece — but something far far simpler.

'I want to read a story that makes me forget I am reading for a competition,' the main short listing judge for Bridport told me. He and his colleagues read anything up to 600 short story entries first pass, and in addition he reads every story his team feel have potential. More than once.

'But how can that happen?' I asked. 'How can you forget you are reading, when you have that lot to get through?!'

'Simple,' he said. 'When all the craft comes together perfectly, it becomes totally invisible. Add that to a good story, one that won't let me go, and I have to read it again, and again.'

So, rule number one, (if there are rules at all) get the technicalities right.

And that means learning. It means hard work, maybe for a long time. It means seeking intelligent feedback from CW teachers or other writers who will give you straight useful responses. Not your beloved partner, or parent, who will just tell you your work is lovely(!) Work with other writers whose writing you admire. Give and receive honest feedback. Read . Read. Read.

Rule number two: research your competition.

How? By reading the successful work from previous years' publications. You wouldn't submit work to a magazine for publication without familiarising yourself with the type of work they prefer. Competitions are no different. You can buy the anthologies from

Fish, Bridport, the Asham Award and many others, and not only have a good read, but you can put on your analytical hat and take those stories apart to see how they were put together.

And, if you entered that particular competition and got nowhere, as I did year on year, you can ask yourself the searching question, 'OK, here's my story, here are the ones that made it. Where did mine fall down?' And learn from an honest comparison.

Rule number three: make your work stand out for the right reasons!

So the reader has 600 stories to read. Your work must be something he/she can't put down. It has to grab from the first sentence or even before. Don't waste the first paragraph on a nice description of the weather. 600 weather forecasts can pall. Think of it as trying to get your reader to swim in a river. Don't let him wander about on the bank, where he might change his mind about jumping in at all. Drop him right into the action, so he has to get taken by the current.

How unique is the 'voice' of the piece? Will it sing in among the hundreds of other voices? Is the world you create different? Compelling the reader to stay and visit?

But before that even, look at the title of your story. How unique is it? If you think it is unique, Google it. If there are a hundred other stories with that title, find another. Make it zippy. The reader might have 50 stories entitled 'The Dream', and one entitled 'Why Cactuses Don't Work'. Which is going to intrigue more?

And speaking as a reader for competitions myself—don't try to make your work stand out by using fluorescent paper,

'Elizabethan' script, flowery borders, a photo of the writer, half naked. (Yes, it happens!) Follow the guidelines, please remember to take your name off the story itself, and make the work look as professional as you can.

Rule number four: stubbornness.

So your work is rejected. The masterpiece didn't get anywhere. Tell me about it. I have over fifty or sixty competition entries in my notebook crossed out with an angry black line. You want to give up, bin the story, shoot the competition judge, find the gin.

But the writing world is littered with potential prize-winners who gave up. Please don't!!

I have a ritual. I read back through the rejected work and apologise to it, because I didn't craft it as well as it could have been crafted. I strip it back to the bones of the story to see . . . how grabbing was this story in the end? How engaging were these characters?

And after adding a large dollop of time to the mix—there is nothing like time to help me see that something I thought stunning is not quite as stunning as I thought—I rewrite. Tinker. And off it goes again.

Believe in yourself and your work. If *you* don't why should anyone else?

And that brings me to the last rule: believe in a little luck.

When you pat your story before sending it off, like a small child on their first day at school, cross your fingers. It may well be that the gods of writing competitions will be shining on you this year.

But whatever happens, if your story ends up bobbing to the top, please also remember that in the end, the final choices are very very tough for the judge. Many of that last fifty entries at a competition like Bridport, for example, could win. Arguably, all the final five or ten are interchangeable. Tracy Chevalier, short story judge in 2007, and Don Paterson, the poetry judge that year, both said exactly the same thing in their addresses to the multitude at the prize giving, and in their judges' reports.

Something to the effect that the last stories and poems are like a bowl full of fruit. There's an orange, a few apples, all different. There are black, red and green grapes- some with pips- there are plums, greengages, passion fruit, grapefruit, a lemon, satsumas, several melons of different colours and flavours, bananas, uglifruit, starfruit, pears, and they are, every single one, unblemished. And you like them all.

The fruit the final judge decides to eat today will not be what they'd have picked yesterday, necessarily, or tomorrow.

Happy Writing, and Good Luck!

(This essay was commissioned by *The New Writer* magazine, and also appears on The Short Story website www.theshortstory.org.uk.)

EPILOGUE

Six Salt Short Story Writers have the final say:

Linda Cracknell
Jay Merill
Carys Davies
David Grubb
Zoe King
Matthew Licht

LINDA CRACKNELL

BALANCING ACT

R ichard Ford calls the short story, 'the high-wire act of literature'. Like poetry, the form involves incredible compression and density, so every word doesn't only count, it must multi-task. As well as moving the narrative forward, dialogue can develop characterisation and add information the reader needs. The description of a setting, seen through the eyes of a character, will be infused by their mood which then doesn't need to be stated. Every detail carries a metaphorical weight. It's not by chance that a bright lamp, a yellow flyer, dollops of honey and the sun are all mentioned in the opening paragraphs of my story, 'The Searching Glance'. What is omitted and implied has to balance this.

Part of the writer's high-wire poise is between intuition and control. I know now when the moment is right to start writing, allowing ideas to accumulate and 'compost' in my mind first. Once I've captured the first element of voice or image, I await the others — characters, ideas or facts, seemingly unconnected. When I saw a winter field crossed by three scarecrows dressed in red overalls, the image was so startling I note-booked it for a story. In the weeks that followed, the other elements appeared and wove themselves around it to become, 'And the Sky was Full of Crows'. I trust my own odd intuition—the subconscious antennae are at work as I listen to the radio or eavesdrop on buses.

I write my first draft 'hot' with a pen and paper, pressing on without re-reading, even if I don't think I know the ending. This is the imaginative journey. The editorial brain chips in as soon as I'm typing. New writers are sometimes surprised that I revise so many times—typically between six and ten, and I don't just mean 'tweaks'. And finally, somewhere towards the end of the process, once I'm certain what I'm writing about, the title declares itself.

FAVOURITE SHORT STORIES

'A Small Good Thing' by Raymond Carver, *Best American Short Stories of the Century*, Ed: John Updike (Houghton Mifflin, 2000)

'Mary in the Mountains' by Christopher Tilghman from *Breaking Into Print* Ed: Dewitt Henry (Beacon Press, 2000)

'Brokeback Mountain' by Annie Proulx from *Close Range* (Harper Perennial, 2000)

'Samphire' by Patrick O'Brien, from *Collected Stories* (Harper Collins, 1994)

'Willing', by Lorrie Moore, from *Birds of America* (Faber and Faber, 1999)

Anything by Alice Munro

IDEAS FOR FURTHER EXPLORATION

ONE

To reveal the hidden depths of your main character, look in their pockets. Don't think too much — write a list quickly, instinctively. You might find something which seems to contradict what you already know and unlocks this character, or upon which the whole story turns.

TWO

Read the first two or three paragraphs of a story you don't know, then do the same at the end. Ask yourself the following questions:

What is the central change that has come about between the beginning and the end?

What kind of thing could create such a change?

What expectation does the title add?

Then read the whole story and see how close your assumptions were. Does the title have any different meaning by the end? This can highlight how writers quickly establish a world and the 'promise' of a story and how they then handle its resolution or frustration.

JAY MERILL

SUPERCHARGED WORDS

Sometimes you can be hit by a word with supercharged energy that enters your head and insists you notice it. I find it's important to stay with such a word to see where it might take you. I tend to write it down because it can disappear again. This has happened to me. I know a word is significant and yet I've lost it. Maybe I was out somewhere and had my everyday mind on other things or maybe I was just falling asleep at the time it hit me. And writing the word down may be the first step in taking the word into the world of the story. It is sealing something; giving recognition. Words which come in this way often end up becoming titles of my stories, I've realised, probably because the title usually expresses the essential thing being said.

This hitting by the supercharged word can happen in a variety of ways. I'll just draw on a few of my own words as examples. *Billie-Ricky.* When I first thought of this word I didn't realise it was a name. It came into my head as a sound doodle one evening when I was on the phone. That whole day I'd felt I had a story coming but I didn't know what it was. It was a bit frustrating and

I was starting to let go of the idea that there was anything, and was just relaxing and talking to the friend. That's when 'Billie-Ricky' entered my mind, and I wrote it down at once. The story wrote itself after that, in a couple of days, with hardly a second draft. *Billie-Ricky* was the key, or the seed which seemed to contain the whole story within itself in miniature. 'Billie-Ricky' was published in Staple Magazine and is one of the stories in my collection *Astral Bodies,* published by Salt in 2007.

I've had word experiences where the outcome has been quite different. The word *precipice* was supercharged for me and I followed where it led me. It turned out not to be the right word in the end but nevertheless it carried me a long way before gently dropping me off like a hitchhiker who'd realised she was going in a different direction after all. It was the brittle 'pr' followed by the swish of the sibilants which made me see those dark gullies between urban blocks of flats, and the flights of birds. *Precipice* was the word which initiated a story which evolved over time, with many different drafts to it. Finally, the precipice became displaced by the pigeon's wing as the central image in my mind. The story became 'God of the Pigeons', which is the title story of my forthcoming collection.

A word I'm currently involved with is *Kootsie.* It popped into my mind the other day to fit an existing image which couldn't seem to express itself unaided. This image has been with me for a year or two. It's a visual memory I have of seeing a man and dog in a park once. I didn't know it was to become a story until *Kootsie* leapt right in and made that clear. *Kootsie* will be the driving force —I can feel the story solidifying and taking shape as I write the word.

FAVOURITE SHORT STORIES

'The Capital of the World' by Ernest Hemingway, from *The 1st 49 Stories* (Scribner, 1936)

'The Dream Lover' by William Boyd, from *The Dream Lover and other stories* (Bloomsbory, 2008)

'Dance of the Happy Shades' by Alice Munro, from *Dance of the Happy Shades and other stories* (McGraw-Hill Ryerson, 1968)

'Death by Landscape' by Margaret Atwood, from *Wilderness Tips* (Anchor Paperbacks, 1991)

'Brokeback Mountain' by Annie Proulx, from *Close Range: Wyoming Stories* (Scribner, 1999)

 IDEAS FOR FURTHER EXPLORATION

1 Think about what is inspiring for you, eg. certain patterns and colour combinations.

2 Sit down in a relaxed state of mind picturing these until they evoke a verbal counterpart.

3 If the word which comes into your mind seems to have a vibrant energy to it, write it down.

4 Try to form an idea of what kind of character or situation could be connected to this word.

5 Develop these by making notes until you see a direction developing.

6 The rhythm of the story should now start to present itself.

7 Begin writing a few sentences in this rhythm until things feel fluid.

8 Your story should begin to unfold.

9 Return to the patterns and colours you first thought of.

10 Repeat this whole process until you feel your story is moving in the way you want it.

CARYS DAVIES

'. . . BEFORE IT DISAPPEARS . . .'

The biggest problem for me when it comes to writing a story —the biggest danger I'd call it—is that I will try to write it in my head before committing it to paper. This is a terrible mistake—my worst habit—and the thing I have to fight against all the time.

I know why I do it: it's because of the fear that the story I've begun to imagine will turn to dust when I write it down, or at the very least fall far short of what I want it to be. But the truth is that the story is much *more* likely to slip through my fingers if I allow myself to keep it in my head. In my head I plan, I sort, I muse over different possibilities—I attempt to figure the whole thing out and invariably what I end up with is the story as I *think* it should be, instead of the story that would have emerged if I'd let it come on the page.

There are things that come when you write that would never come when you think. When you write quickly without suppressing anything, before you know it, there it is: something you've never thought of, haven't planned, but which begins to shape

238

whatever you've begun with—an image or a name or a memory or a scrap of conversation—into something like a story.

I try to write very quickly, pushing on when I come to an apparent dead-end, because so often that's *precisely* the moment I'll end up setting down the line that takes me by surprise—that makes the whole story 'swivel', and gives it its real direction and its meaning. It might be the moment when I suddenly realise who's telling the story or *why* they have to tell it; it might be the moment when a character does something unexpected but entirely logical and necessary—the thing that gives the tale that elusive combination of surprise and inevitability that is the short story's most delicious pleasure.

So every day, in the morning, I try not to think about things for too long, because it's dangerous. Raymond Carver understood this—he spoke of the need, with a short story, to get 'in and out' very quickly—and so did Katherine Mansfield, who wrote that 'It's always a kind of race to get in as much as one can before it *disappears.*' (her italics)

When things aren't working—when I haven't yet discovered what the story is about and why it's worth telling—I try various things to help myself out. I'll write the story from the point of view of all the characters in the story, or begin at what until now I've thought of as the end, or in the middle, or somewhere else along the way. But there are times when I'm so frustrated or angry or bored with my own writing that I'll take someone else's from the shelf, something perfect like 'The Means of Escape' by Penelope Fitzgerald or Anton Chekov's 'A Lady with a Dog' and copy it out, word for word, in the hope that something—a sense of timing and movement, a way of saying neither too much nor too little—will eventually sink in. And even if it doesn't, at least in the course of a bad day's work, I can enjoy the illusion of having written something really good.

Other stories I return to again and again include John Cheever's 'The Country Husband', Annie Proulx's 'The Half-Skinned Steer', Bernard Malamud's 'The Magic Barrel' and, more recently, Cormac McCarthy's great novel *The Road* because it strikes me every time I read it that it possesses—with its intense and beautifully rendered present set between a cataclysmic past and a tentative, tantalizing future—all the qualities of a brilliant short story.

REFERENCE BOOKS

Mansfield, Katherine. *Letters and Journals* (Penguin, 1977)

'The Means of Escape' by Penelope Fitzgerald from *The Means of Escape* (Flamingo, 2000)

'A Lady with a Dog' by Anton Chekov from *The Russian Master and Other Stories* (Oxford University Press, 1999)

'The Country Husband' by John Cheever from *The Best American Short Stories of the Century* (Houghton Mifflin, 1999)

'The Half-Skinned Steer' by Annie Proulx from *The Best American Short Stories of the Century* (Houghton Mifflin, 1999)

'The Magic Barrel' by Bernard Malamud from *The Magic Barrel* (Chatto & Windus, 1979)

McCarthy, Cormac. *The Road* (Vintage, 2007)

FAVOURITE SHORT STORIES

'O City of Broken Dreams' by John Cheever from *The Granta Book of the American Short Story* (Granta, 1992)

'A Piece of News' by Eudora Welty from *Selected Stories of Eudora Welty* (The Modern Library, 1971)

'The Man of the House' by Frank O'Connor from *50 Great Short Stories* (Bantam Books, 1952)

'The Lottery' by Shirley Jackson from *50 Great Short Stories* (Bantam Books, 1952)

'An Anxious Man' by James Lasdun from *It's Beginning to Hurt* (Jonathan Cape, 2009)

'Pilgrims' by Julie Orringer from *How to Breathe Underwater* (Penguin, 2005)

'The Father' by Leonid Dobychin from *Russian Short Stories from Pushkin to Buida* (Penguin, 2005)

'Winter Storm' by Bernard MacLaverty from *Matters of Life & Death* (Vintage, 2007)

IDEAS FOR FURTHER EXPLORATION

I don't really use exercises to write but one thing that comes to mind is a picture a friend sent me a couple of years ago. It's called *The Last Inn by the Town Gate*, by Vasili Perov, 1868. It's a murky scene, lit only by the windows of an inn and outside, on a sledge, there's a dark shawled figure. I was so struck by it — by the warm light coming from the inn and the lonely figure out in the snow — that I began to write about it, and continued to do so, on and off, for about eighteen months, imagining different explanations for the scene, but no story ever really took shape until, eventually, after leaving it aside for several more months, it turned into a story called 'The Travellers', published in the 2009 *Willesden Herald* short story competition anthology *New Short Stories 3* (Pretend Genius Press, 2009).

Go and find a painting, a postcard, a photograph that intrigues you. And write about it. Again and again, over time. What's going on here? Why?

DAVID GRUBB

DANCING ON GLASS

ESSENCE

T he essence of short fiction is brevity, the fast flight of ideas, a suggestion that there might be more to come. It is more jazz than chamber music, more tango than waltz. Sometimes it is like dancing on glass.

This urgency, pace, cutting-edge quality is closer to the poem in its energy level than other forms of narrative, with a spirit of searching and not necessarily finding.

There are several basic elements in writing short fiction; the voice of the story teller, pace changes, the anarchy of soft or savage ideas, the urge to see something in a different way. It could be expressed as power running on the page.

The most compelling short stories also have traces of escapade and jeopardy.

We seem to live in short fictions, we try to hold on but keep letting go. A good short story is likewise not so much a settlement as a surge. It has to do this in a very short space of time. If you dance on glass for too long cracks will appear.

ESTABLISHING VOICE

In tutoring creative writing classes the challenge has rarely been about a lack of ideas or understanding the basic way stories are told; it has been about exposing the story to an array of new ideas and letting go so that the narrative begins to have a life of its own. It is about a way of telling a story that transforms the story. It is about finding things beneath the surface. It is about letting the story tell you things as you write it and surpassing the opening idea.

CONSTRUCTIONS

Titles: the title is vital, as is the opening paragraph. If an expectation is not set up in the mind of the reader within a few words the reader will not engage.

Telling: the sound of the story, the way the story is told, the subject matter—these are the elements which will attract and hold a reader who will naturally be subjective in terms of taste.

Layering: depth and a sense of progression are essential in creating the 'aboutness' of the narrative and energising its nature.

Short: a short story is not like a chapter in a novel. It is a lake, not an ocean. It is a song, not an opera. Contrast J G Ballard, Philip O'Ceallaigh, Paul Yoon, Joyce Carol Oates, William Trevor.

Endings: the art of the ending is to deliver the reader to a place where all that has gone before is enhanced, transformed. Often it is the very last sentence that achieves this sense of wholeness and closure. Contrast D.H. Lawrence, Lorrie Moore, Alice Munro.

 IDEAS FOR FURTHER EXPLORATION

ONE

In order to find a specific voice for each piece of work and establish its sound from the start, I use an exercise called *A Way Of Saying Things*. Begin with a list of story titles/ideas which have a hint of colour, mood, noise about them. Examples might be:

- A gathering of questions without answers
- A letter in your head that will never be sent
- A field where there are voices but no people
- A funeral at which the dead wife says the amens
- A story about a man called Grass
- A tramp called John Clare
- The day we got drunk on apple pie

See how many different stories these titles evoke, what sort of voice and writing style they suggest. Let them encourage you to tell a story in a different way and march off the map.

One writer recently termed this approach *tightrope writing.*

TWO

This exercise focusses on identities. It assists in expanding subject matter, writing style and departing from comfort zones and also takes advantage of our image-driven culture. This was originally devised within a writing group, the members of which were dedicated to the idea that storis coming out of a real life events, or based upon them, had limitations in terms of building fictions.

Working with images from newspapers and magazines, picture postcards and posters and restricting the writing entirely to dialogue, you are encouraged to enter the image, become present in its story. To do this convincingly you have to adopt another being, a different way of telling, a compelling voice. You begin to change the story from documentary into the extraordinary.

FAVOURITE SHORT STORIES

Having written novels, poetry and short stories for some time, I increasingly respect the nature and importance of the short story form. The stories that now reside in my soul are totally different and demand different ways of reading and perceiving. They all have moments of enthralling exposure, wonder and revelation. You feel that each writer has just put in place a section of a massive stained glass window, filled with a narrative of radiant light and surprising exposures:

'The Rocking Horse Winner' by D H Lawrence is online here: www.dowse.com

'The Things They Carried' by Tim O'Brien from *Best American Short Stories of the Century*, Ed: John Updike (Houghton Mifflin, 2000)

'The Hummingbird That Lived Through Winter' by William Saroyan, from *Eco Fiction* Ed: John Stadler (Pocket Books, 1978)

'The Loss' by David Constantine, from *Under the Dam* (Comma Press, 2008)

'My Dead Brother Comes to America' by Alexander Godin, from *Best American Short Stories of the Century*, Ed: John Updike (Houghton Mifflin, 2000)

ZOE KING

BUT WHAT IF YOUR CHARACTER WON'T TALK TO YOU?

So, you have your character, you can see her clearly in your mind's eye, you can sense her concerns, she has allowed you to listen in to her thoughts and her way of thinking them, you can almost reach out and touch her, and yet . . . like a horse clinging to the safety of the stalls, she 'refuses' when it comes to sharing her story.

This, I suspect is the dilemma of many short story writers, particularly those who write intuitively, trusting that once they have the voice, the character, the rest will follow organically, and a more or less fully formed story will emerge. And very often of course, it will. Those who have internalised the craft know and trust that this is how it happens, even if their starting point differs from that of other writers.

As a short story writer, I wholly believe that character is key. Even where I have a setting, or a possible story scenario, that scenario cannot come to life until I have fully grasped its character and allowed him or her to tell the tale. I can't force character onto situation because that 'top-down' imposition will always feel contrived.

Let me give you an example. Some time ago, I was in Ibiza with a friend when she showed me a tiny open-air chapel set into a hillside. I went back and back to that little chapel because it fascinated me so, and as I sat and absorbed it, a character presented herself, and slowly, her story emerged. She told me her name, and while I accepted it in the first instance, I later found myself wrestling with it because another name, that of her partner, threatened to take precedence. Hers arose naturally, his less so, the result of a derivation, but because I liked his, (it was unusual, whereas hers was commonplace) I decided to stick with his and change hers, because they were too alike, and might confuse the reader.

When I set to committing the story to paper, the chapel, with its white curved walls and its naturally occurring carob trees took precedence because that setting was my introduction to my character. My character however refused to play, regardless of how seductive the setting. First of all, I'd had the gall to discard the name she had first given me, and then, if that wasn't enough, I'd also had the temerity to present her in relation to the setting instead of the other way round. Yes, she came via place, but her *story* was what mattered, and while the chapel setting certainly spoke to theme, it wasn't inevitable, or irreplaceable.

I suspect that very often, if your character is refusing to speak to you, it's because you are *imposing* elements of the story, rather than allowing them to arise naturally. Character is to voice is to theme is to plot is to story. Learn to trust that left to his or her own devices, your character *will* deliver.

FAVOURITE SHORT STORIES

'What We Talk about When We Talk about Love' by Raymond Carver from *Where I'm Calling From: The Selected Stories* (The Harvill Press, 1995)

'The Higgler' by A E Coppard from *The Story and Its Writer: An Introduction to Short Fiction* (St Martin's Press, 1983)

'The Overcoat' by Nikolai Gogol from *The Collected Tales of Nikolai Gogol* (Granta Books, 2003)

'Woman in a Lampshade' by Elizabeth Jolley from *Woman in a Lampshade* (Penguin, 1983)

'Death by Landscape' by Margaret Atwood from *Margaret Atwood Omnibus: Wilderness Tips, Cat's Eye* (Little, Brown and Company, 1999)

'Brokeback Mountain' by Annie Proulx from *Close Range: Wyoming Stories* (Fourth Estate, 1999)

 IDEAS FOR FURTHER EXPLORATION

ONE

Google baby names and spend some time looking at the lists for both girls and boys. Don't rush this, savour the names, until one of them speaks to you. Names carry resonance, some more than others, and it's often possible for a story to arise purely from a name.

TWO

Think about people you have known who had nicknames. Why did they attract those names? Dream up a character and give him or her a nickname rather than a name, and allow the associated trait to take you into a story.

MATTHEW LICHT

ICEBERG LETTUCE: WHY I WRITE, AND A LITTLE BIT OF 'HOW'

Read people a story you wrote and someone will always ask whether it's true.

If you bake a pie, someone wants to know if you made the crust from scratch.

Some people like stories and pies better if the person responsible looks them in the eye and says of course it's a true story, of course I harvested wheat and milled grist before I attempted the rhubarb cobbler.

I learned to write stories in front of grade school kids and readers of a publication skewed towards breast obsession. Jam a ballpoint firmly into nostrils to establish interest. Don't let attention waver for the space of a tired phrase or even a word out of place, or you're dead, as far as the story goes.

Swimming was the only thing that ever came naturally. It made sense to move through the water *with* the water, like the water, without struggle or violence. A teacher said, 'He's slow at everything else, so . . .' What I picked up from swimming is, don't think about what you're doing. Don't look at what everyone else is doing. Don't hesitate. Or you lose.

A person swimming has no choice but to be in the water. And you move faster, more easily, under the surface. But it's hard to breathe.

Judo is a sport I loved but wasn't good at. Broke my heart. Broke my leg. Judo's heavily counter-intuitive. If your opponent pulls, don't pull back. Same if he pushes. Move with him, a little further than he expects or wants you to go. This has a destabilizing, unbalancing effect. Flip him across the room, land on him like a cheap, suffocating suit. Attempt a sloppy throw, make your intentions known, down you go.

Trap drums were another rich source of frustration. Seems easy, at first. No notes. Whack tubs like a chimp. Improvise freely like those crazy jazz cats. What a dream. Only you have to devolve into an amoeba, annihilate your ego, sacrifice everything else and humbly submerge yourself in rhythm. I wasn't willing go all the way, and that's the only thing that matters.

For many years after I quit, I tried to write about what drums mean. The story was exorcism.

I'm not a drummer. I'm a writer.

I have to keep reminding myself. Too easy to get distracted. Writers can live more or less like everyone else, but should be careful what they get fully involved with. Suffering enters the picture. Some people might not like being turned into characters. Others don't want their problems and quirks presented as literary entertainment. You can't make *everything* up. Sometimes a story comes from a spontaneous mental picture. You see a person doing something unusual, an odd combination of people in an unlikely setting, wonder what's going on, what happened. Sometimes a name is enough.

J.D. Salinger's stories suggest nearly forgotten worlds, a way of being children and adults which might be better than what we know, what we've got. Truman Capote managed the same difficult trick with glittering, spectacular effect.

Ernest Hemingway gave away a professional secret when he conjured iceberg tips afloat on dark, unfathomably cold water.

Unjustly neglected John O'Hara described an athlete's desire for satisfying evacuation the day after a match. Victory and medals are fine, lightness is better. Release is made more difficult, if not impossible, by the effort expended.

Thomas Mann got up at dawn every day, took a cold bath and got to work.

CONTRIBUTORS' NOTES

LANE ASHFELDT

Lane Ashfeldt's short fiction has been widely published in anthologies, writing journals and online literary spaces, and has won her several awards. She is also known as a fiction editor: she is co-founder of the fiction website Pulp Net www.pulp.net and has edited the anthology *Down the Angel and Up Holloway* (Pulp Net, 2006). She currently teaches Advanced Creative Writing with the Open University. A collection of her own short fiction is on the way, and recent stories appear in the anthologies *Punk Fiction* (Portico, 2009) and *What We Were Thinking Just Before The End* (The Green Press, 2009). More at www.ashfeldt.com

ELIZABETH BAINES

Elizabeth Baines is a prize-winning writer of prose fiction and plays for radio and stage. Her short stories have been published widely in magazines and anthologies including *Best Short Stories from Stand Magazine* (Methuen). Her story collection, *Balancing on the Edge of the World*, was published by Salt in 2007, and Salt publish her novel *Too Many Magpies* (October 2009). She has taught Creative Writing to adult education classes and in schools, and has had periods teaching fiction-writing on BA courses at Bolton Institute and the University of Manchester. She is the author of the chapter 'Innovative Fiction and the Novel' in *The Creative Writing Handbook* (Macmillan) ed. John Singleton and Mary Luckhurst, and of 'Naming the Fictions' in *Feminist Literary Theory* (Blackwell) ed. Mary Eagleton. With Ailsa Cox she founded and edited the acclaimed short story magazine, *Metropolitan* (1992-97). http://www.elizabethbaines.com

ELAINE CHIEW

Elaine Chiew is a Malaysian-born writer. Now recently moved to Hong Kong, she was the winner of the 2008 Bridport Prize for fiction. Her short stories have appeared in various literary journals and anthologies—most recently in *One World: An Global Anthology of Short Stories* (New Internationalist, 2009). She is currently at work on a novel and a collection of short stories.

LINDA CRACKNELL

Linda Cracknell has been a teacher of English in Zanzibar, worked for environmental charity WWF, and was writer-in-residence at Hugh MacDiarmid's last home near Biggar. She now lives in Highland Perthshire. Her short fiction has appeared in magazines and journals, been broadcast on BBC radio, and was previously collected in *Life Drawing*, published in 2000. Her latest collection, *The Searching Glance* was published by Salt in 2008. She writes drama for BBC Radio 4 and is now writing essays about walks which follow human stories in 'wild' places.

CARYS DAVIES

Carys Davies' short stories have won prizes in national and international competitions, including the Bridport, Asham, Orange/Harpers & Queen and Fish. They have been published in magazines and anthologies and broadcast on BBC Radio 4. Her debut collection of short stories *Some New Ambush* (Salt 2007) was short-listed for the 2009 Roland Mathias Prize, long-listed for the 2008 Wales Book of the Year Prize and was a Finalist in the 2008 Calvino Prize in the US. She lives in Lancaster with her husband and four children.

DAVID GAFFNEY

David Gaffney is from Manchester. He is the author of *Sawn Off Tales* (Salt 2006), *Aromabingo* (Salt 2007), *Never Never* (Tindal Street 2008), 'Buildings Crying Out', a story using lost cat posters (Lancaster Litfest 2009), *23 Stops To Hull*, stories about junctions on the M62 (Humbermouth festival 2009) *Rivers Take Them,* a set of short operas with composer Ailis Ni Riain (BBC Radio 3, 2008.) and *Destroy PowerPoint*, stories in PowerPoint format (Edinburgh Festival Fringe 2009). His new collection of microfiction, *The Half-Life of Songs*, will be published by Salt in 2010.

MARIAN GARVEY

Marian Garvey won First Prize in the Asham Award (2007). She has previously been shortlisted for other short story awards and her stories have appeared in various anthologies and on Radio 4. Marian is currently working on her first novel with Arts Council funding.

VANESSA GEBBIE

Vanessa Gebbie's short fiction has won over forty awards, including prizes at Bridport, Fish (twice), Per Contra (USA), the *Daily Telegraph* and the *Willesden Herald*, from final judges such as Zadie Smith, Tracy Chevalier, Michael Collins and Colum McCann.

She is a freelance writing teacher working with adult groups, at literary festivals and with school students. Her work with disadvantaged adults led to the publication of two anthologies of their writing: *Roofless* and *Refuge* (QueenSpark Publishing 2007). In 2009 she was invited to contribute to *A Field Guide to Writing Flash Fiction* (Rose Metal Press USA), a creative writing textbook that received a coveted starred review from *Publisher's Weekly*.

Many of her prize-winning stories are brought together for the first time in her collection *Words from a Glass Bubble* (Salt, 2008). A second collection, *Ed's Wife and Other Creatures,* is forthcoming from Salt. She is Welsh and lives in East Sussex. For more information, see: www.vanessagebbie.com

DAVID H W GRUBB

David H W Grubb has published poetry, novels, novellas, radio plays and short stories. His most recent poetry collection, *The Man Who Spoke To Owls,* was published by Shearsman in 2009. A short story collection, *Hullabaloo,* is forthcoming from Salt, and a novella will be published in 2010. His short stories have appeared in

Horizon, Geometer and *The Matthew's House Project, Stand, With* and the 2007 Bridport anthology.

TANIA HERSHMAN

Half of the stories in Tania Hershman's first collection, *The White Road and Other Stories* (Salt, 2008), www.TheWhiteRoadAndOther-Stories.com) are flash fiction. She is the European regional winner of the 2008 Commonwealth Broadcasting Association's 600-word short story contest, joint winner of the 2008 Biscuit Publishing Flash Fiction competition, and winner of Creating Reality's 2nd 300-word story competition. Her short and flash stories have been widely published online and in print and broadcast on BBC Radio 4. Tania is founder and editor of The Short Review (www.TheShortReview.com), an online literary journal devoted to reviewing short story collections. A former science journalist, born in London, Tania, who has just moved to Bristol after 15 years in Jerusalem, Israel, is a full-time writer and teacher of creative writing. For more about her writing visit: www.Tania-Hershman.com and also her blog, TaniaWrites: www.titania-writes.blogspot.com.

TOBIAS HILL

Selected as one of the country's Next Generation poets, shortlisted for the 2004 *Sunday Times* Young Writer of the Year and named by the *TLS* as one of the best young writers in the country, Tobias Hill is one of the leading British writers of his generation. His award-winning collections of poetry are *Year of the Dog, Midnight in the City of Clocks* and *Zoo*. His fiction has been published to acclaim in many countries. AS Byatt has observed that 'There is no other voice today quite like this.'

ALEX KEEGAN

Alex Keegan began writing seriously in 1992, publishing five mystery novels before switching to serious short fiction. He has been published widely in print and on the web and been awarded more than a dozen first prizes for his fiction as well as three Bridport Prizes. Many of his prize-winning stories have been collected in *Ballistics* (Salt, 2009). Born in Wales with an Irish mother, he now lives and writes in Newbury, England with his second wife and two teenage children. He runs a tough internet writing school, 'Boot Camp Keegan'.

ZOE KING

Zoe King's award-winning short stories have appeared in literary magazines and anthologies in the UK and overseas. Founder editor of *BuzzWords*, and former editor of *Cadenza*, a collection of her work is forthcoming from Salt. A regular workshop leader, she has been teaching creative writing for many years, was a panellist at the Geneva Writers Conference in 2001, taught briefly at the much-missed BBC Get Writing site, and has taught her own creativity project, Journeys to Voice, both online and at writers' retreats since 2005. She currently works as a freelance writer and editor, and is Vice Chair of The Society of Women Writers & Journalists. See more at her website: www.zoeking.com and at www.swwj.co.uk

MATTHEW LICHT

Matthew Licht's collection of short stories, *The Moose Show* (Salt, 2007) was nominated for the Frank O'Connor Prize. A second collection, *Justine, Joe & The Zen Garbageman* is forthcoming, also from Salt. Matthew Licht's stories have been in *Ambit*, *Litro*, *Reality*, *Tom's Voice*, *The Writing Site* and many underground publications.

ALISON MACLEOD

Alison MacLeod was raised in Canada and has lived in England since 1987. Her short stories have been widely published in a variety of literary magazines and collections, and broadcast on the BBC. Her short story collection, *Fifteen Modern Tales of Attraction*, was published by Hamish Hamilton/Penguin in 2007. In 2008, she was the recipient of the Society of Authors' Olive Cook Award for Short Fiction, while her collection was nominated for the International Frank O'Connor Award for Short Fiction and the 2009 Book to Talk About Award. She has also published two critically acclaimed novels, *The Changeling* (1996) and *The Wave Theory of Angels* (2005). Her next novel will be published by Hamish Hamilton and is set in Brighton, where she now lives. Alongside her writing, she is Professor of Contemporary Fiction at the University of Chichester where she teaches on the MA in Creative Writing. For further information about her work, please see www.alison-macleod.com.

PAUL MAGRS

Paul Magrs was born in 1969 in the North East of England. He has published novels for adults and teens. His first collection of stories, *Playing Out* was published by Vintage in 1997. His second, *Twelve Stories* was published twleve years later by Salt in 2009. He lectured in English Literature and Creative Writing at UEA for seven years and now teaches at Manchester Metropolitan University.

ADAM MAREK

Adam Marek's short story collection, *Instruction Manual for Swallowing* (Comma Press) was longlisted for the Frank O'Connor Prize — the biggest prize in the world for a collection of short stories. His stories have also appeared in *Prospect* magazine and various anthologies including *The New Uncanny* and *When It Changed* from Comma Press, two Bridport Prize collections, and the British Council's *New Writing 15*. He is working on his first novel. www.adammarek.co.uk

JAY MERILL

Jay Merill's short story collection *Astral Bodies* was published by Salt in 2007 and her second collection, *God of the Pigeons* is forthcoming from Salt. Jay is currently working on a novel, assisted by an Arts Council Award. She is co-organiser of the spoken word event Ride the Word.

GRAHAM MORT

Graham was winner of the 2007 Bridport prize for short fiction, and his collection of short stories, *Touch*, will be published by Seren in 2009. He teaches Creative Writing at Lancaster University and has worked extensively for the British Council in Africa on the Crossing Borders writing project, which he designed and led. He is currently developing Radiophonics, a radio-writing project that promotes short fiction in Uganda and Nigeria, in partnership with the British Council and local broadcasters.

Graham has published eight books of poetry and has won a number of awards for his work, including prizes in the Arvon and Cheltenham Poetry Competition and a major Eric Gregory Award. His most recent poetry collection is *Visibility: New & Selected Poems* (Seren). He has broadcast fiction, drama and poetry for BBC radio and his short stories have previously appeared in many literary magazines.

NUALA NÍ CHONCHÚIR

Fiction writer and poet born in Dublin, Ireland in 1970. Her third short fiction collection *Nude* was published by Salt in September 2009. Her first two collections *The Wind Across the Grass* (2004 & 2009) and *To The World of Men, Welcome* (2005) were published by Arlen House. Nuala was chosen by the *Irish Times* as a writer to watch in 2009; she has won many short fiction prizes including the Cúirt New Writing Prize, RTÉ radio's Francis MacManus Award, the inaugural Jonathan Swift Award and the Cecil Day Lewis Award. She was recently shortlisted for the European Prize for Literature and she was one of four winners of the Templar Poetry Pamphlet and Collection competition. Her pamphlet *Portrait of the Artist with a Red Car* will be published by Templar in November 2009. Nuala's first novel *You* will be published by New Island in 2010. Website: www.nualanichonchuir.com

SARAH SALWAY

Sarah Salway has won many prizes for her short stories, collected in *Leading the Dance* (bluechrome), and was the judge for the 2008 short story competition for *The New Writer* magazine. She is the RLF Fellow at the London School of Economics and the author of two novels, *Something Beginning With* and *Tell Me Everything* (Bloomsbury). Sarah lives in London and Kent, and is currently working on her second short story collection.

CATHERINE SMITH

Catherine Smith writes prose, poetry and drama. Many of her short stories (several prize-winning) have been published in the UK, and two have been broadcast on BBC Radio 4's *Afternoon Reading* slot. In June 2004 she was listed as one of the Next Generation poets by the Poetry Book Society/*Guardian* — 'the twenty most exciting poets to have published a first collection in the last ten years' — by a panel chaired by the poet laureate, Andrew Motion. Her first short poetry collection, *The New Bride*, was short-listed for the Forward Prize for Best First Collection 2001, and her first full collection, *The Butcher's Hands*, was awarded a Poetry Book Society Recommendation. Her latest poetry collection, *Lip*, was published by Smith/Doorstop in November 2007.She is a member of the National Association of Writers in Education and runs poetry/prose workshops in schools and colleges.

CHIKA UNIGWE

Chika Unigwe is a Nigerian-born author. She has a Ph.D in Literature from the University of Leiden in the Netherlands. Her debut novel, *De Feniks* was published in 2005 by Meulenhoff and Manteau (of Amsterdam and Antwerp) and was shortlisted for the Vrouw en Kultuur debuutprijs for the best first novel by a female writer. She is also the author of two children's books published by Macmillan, London. She has published short fiction in several anthologies including *Wasafiri* (of the University of London), *Moving Worlds* (of the University of Leeds), Voices of the University of Wisconsin and *Okike* of the University of Nigeria, and *One World* (New Internationalist, 2009). In 2003, she was shortlisted for the Caine Prize for African Fiction. In 2004, she won the BBC Short Story Competition and a Commonwealth Short Story Competition award. In the same year, her short story made the top 10 of the Million Writers' Award for best online fiction. In 2005, she won the 3rd prize in the Equiano Fiction Contest. She lives in Turnhout, Belgium.

CLARE WIGFALL

Clare Wigfall was born in Greenwich during the summer of 1976. She spent her early childhood in Berkeley, California before returning to London. She has since lived in Manchester, Prague, Granada, Norwich, Ceske Budejovice, and now Berlin. Her first collection of stories *The Loudest Sound and Nothing* was published by Faber and Faber in September 2007 to critical acclaim. The following summer she was awarded the BBC National Short Story Award, the world's richest prize for a short story. Her work has been published in *Prospect*, *A Public Space*, *New Writing 10*, *Tatler*, *The*

Dublin Review, and commissioned for BBC Radio 4. She is currently working on a new collection of short stories, and has recently finished a book for children called *Has Anyone Seen My Chihuahua?*

ACKNOWLEDGEMENTS

One day, you receive a message—via email or phone— asking you to give of yourself for very little return other than 'literary riches in heaven', from the editor of a book as yet untitled. There is no list of other contributors, so far. But this book will be a celebration of all you love about the short story form. It will be a chance to pass on your passion to the next generation of writers, to share your hard-won insights about craft. And you are invited to be honest about your own processes—to talk about how words flow and how they don't. To expose yourself as a human being. What utter cheek. How impossible to say no!

To every contributor. Thank you. To those who hold often very high-ranking teaching posts, I bow, and acknowledge how very lucky are those students who pass through your sphere of influ- ence. And to the few here who have yet to teach formally—I'd say get on with it. You are a natural. And to contributor Zoe King, a heartfelt thank you for her proofreading skills.

To all those who read the manuscript and gave your endorse- ments. To have the backing of the Bridport Prize, the Frank O'Connor Award, the National Association of Writers in

Education, the Asham Trust and the Fish Prize, as well as creative writing tutors and writers—is an indicator that we did something right, here. Thank you.

To Jen and Chris Hamilton-Emery of Salt Publishing, who work hard against the odds, for the love of the short story and poetry, all their books and those writers they believe ought to be heard. Thank you.

And to my novel in progress—my twelve men and the storyteller who sat patiently in the shadows for months waiting to be allowed to speak, while I sidelined them and worked on *Short Circuit*, bless you.

Lightning Source UK Ltd.
Milton Keynes UK
UKOW011155180911

178817UK00001B/6/P